Dec. 25, 2008

To Michael

Best Wishes

Enjoy

Fred Biebel

Mr B

I

Path of a Patriot
The Political Journey of Mr. B.

Frederick K. Biebel

IN COLLABORATION WITH
Susan Heller

ISBN 978-0-6152-3665-0

First Edition: July 2008

This book is dedicated with love and pride
to my ever supportive family,
and in particular to Violet,
my beautiful wife of 57 years.

ACKNOWLEDGEMENTS

This book has been a labor of love for me as well as a gift to my loving family. Work on this manuscript began as early as 2003, when I was urged by family members and friends to write about my experience.

You might say the book, like a life, is a work in progress, and it is my hope that my children, grandchildren and great-grandchildren will add to it with their own stories and future books. As early as 1950, my late mother and I spent a week in Falmouth, Massachusettes researching family genealogy. This book is a continuation of that experience and a celebration of my larger family as much as of my own work in politics.

My original goal was simply to leave a brief history for my children, grandchildren, and great-grandchildren, to share with them a glimpse into some of the remarkable people and situations I was fortunate enough to encounter in my career. Along the way, as the work progressed and the cast of characters in the book grew, it occurred to all of us that this manuscript might be of larger interest. I will leave that to the reader to judge.

I wish to thank some of the many people who helped me put this book together.

I remain grateful to my daughter-in-law, Yvonne, my son, Kevin for their support and their efforts to move this book along. My daughter Karen Biebel Sutera was instrumental and tireless in typing the early manuscript and moving the entire story along.

Thanks also go to my cousin Nancy Hatch Warner, whose continuous correspondence aided Jim Curry, a South Carolina archeologist. He played an unwitting and crucial role in bringing the book to conclusion when he discovered a broken gravestone in a salvage yard. His discovery reconnected us with family history and brought the story full circle. I am very grateful for his respect for history and consideration for our family. Likewise, Brian Sweeney of North Carolina also played a role in preserving the gravestone and linking our family to its past.

Thanks also go to my friend Attorney Norman Liss, who provided legal assistance on the Magna Carta tour and much sage advice on this manuscript. My lifelong friend John W. Hughes also made valuable suggestions and changes as well as Dr. Donald Wetmore, noted public speaker and consultant, who, for the better part of two years we sat down together on Thursday evenings and talked the book out. I remain deeply grateful for the gift of his friendship.

I also have been fortunate to work with the creative team that helped assemble this book. Susan Heller, my collaborator, brought considerable writing and organization skills to the manuscript; Andy Glad was a trusted advisor in addition to being an excellent graphic designer; Brian Wallace served as a writing consultant on the project, and Avril Westmoreland as manuscript proofreader.

As we approach yet another national election, we have much to celebrate in our families, our political system and our freedom. This book is an expression of some of those values and a tribute to all those who love our country and work together to make a difference.

Frederick K. Biebel

June 2008

Table of Contents

XII

FORWARD

What in the world is a lifelong, dyed-in-the-wool, bleeding, close to hemorrhaging liberal heart Democrat like me, doing writing a paean to a staunch, straight-arrow Republican who literally flinches when he hears the name of Hillary Clinton? I may be a Democrat, but I know quality when I see it. And Fred Biebel is one of the good guys.

I'm also someone who respects traditions. When you have Captain Henry Biebel, Fred's great-grandfather from the Civil War making sure his obituary would include the statement that he had been "a staunch Republican all his life," that piece is securely in place.

Fred's father continued the family trajectory, spending many a year yowling about Harry Truman and how he sold us out at Yalta, and railing unrelentingly about Woodrow Wilson screwing up the League of Nations, so I can certainly see that consistency counts.

That and the fact that the man has devoted sixty years of his life to a cause he believes in and a country he continues to fight for in every way possible. He is a man of honor, great integrity and more energy than any fourteen people I know put together. He played by the rules and practiced the intelligent use of civil discourse, whereby people from both sides of the aisle *and* the press fought furiously for their individual causes, then got together socially to learn about each other as human beings.

Most importantly, Fred did something about his political convictions. *He acted on them* and, in so doing, helped to change the very history of this country. That's a hell of a lot more than most people do in service to their beliefs, so I figure we owe him and all the old-school Republicans one. They are a special breed: men like Gerald Ford, Ronald Reagan, and Prescott Bush. Whether you agreed with their policies and politics, you had to know they loved this country fiercely and devoted their lives to it.

You will see that, although you may not recognize his name as you do those I just mentioned, Fred Biebel is very much a man in their league. And it is my sincere conviction that if we don't teach the up-and-coming generations how you evolve a man or woman of that stature and standing, we are goners for sure.

We no longer have the rock solid foundations provided by growing up within extended families. We don't have neighborhoods where kids run free in and out of one another's houses and know they can be disciplined or corrected by any one of the adults in their world.

There isn't a context for learning about the need to depend on one another and to take into account others in trouble. For people like Fred, it's just what you did. You looked out for each other. You had to. He has passed that sensibility on to two more generations who, in their turn, are teaching what they were taught.

So here--for those who want to know what it took to evolve a man who would be at the very heart of national politics, who would keep his word and fight the good fight--is an account of the making of a Kingmaker. Who decided he need not be king.

CHAPTER 1
An Offer He Couldn't Refuse

Sometimes in life, you get an offer you just can't refuse – not because of intimidation or financial reward, but because you simply know it's the right thing to do.

You ponder the deal, mull it over in your brain, weigh the pros and cons. Then you take it outside of yourself and you talk it over with family, friends and colleagues. Listening to their concerns and objections somehow helps clarify and strengthen that internal voice that is saying, contrary to all appearances, you have to go with your gut and say, "Yes! I'll do it!"

That is what happened when, in the late fall of 1979, which found him in the middle of a political career, he was asked to work for Ronald Reagan instead of George Bush in the campaign for the Republican Presidential nomination in 1980. A mere three years after calling Reagan a disaster for Connecticut.

Things had changed since he'd made that declaration. Fred had learned a lot during his work as Chairman. He had developed many new friends and contacts on both sides of the aisle. He'd learned more about Reagan, as well, the kinds of things he stood for, his sense of what he wanted to do for the country.

Fred and John Sears, Reagan's campaign manager, conversed often about all kinds of party business. But from the start, Fred knew this conversation was different.

"Hey Fred, it's John. I have a question for you."

"Sure, go ahead."

"How do you feel about Ronald Reagan?"

No small talk, none of the social amenities, straight to the point.

Fred replied, "Well John, quite honestly, I've developed a warm spot in my heart for him. I think he deserves a shot at the nomination."

"That's what I was hoping to hear. Listen, I'm going to have Charlie Black get in touch with you."

Charlie Black was a campaign strategist from the Washington/Virginia area who had been active with Reagan in the earlier campaign against Ford.

At that time, Charlie was a very popular guy in Washington who later formed Black, Manaforte & Stone, a public affairs company in Alexandria, Virginia.

In a slightly torqued version of the axiom, "all roads lead to Washington," back in 1971 Fred was Nicholas Panuzio's campaign manager in his bid for Mayor of Bridgeport, a city that hadn't elected a Republican Mayor for forty years. Panuzio served two terms. He later was appointed by President Ford to head up the GSA in Washington and eventually joined the firm of Black, Manaforte & Stone.

According to Fred, "Charlie was a politician's politician. A real savvy guy, smooth, good talker, bright, knew politics inside and out. An expert strategist, a guy you can trust. I've seen him recently, we were together at the White House at a Christmas Party in 2007. A delightful guy, I think he is still a consultant for Fox News and see him on TV all the time."

Returning to 1979, within a few days, Charlie Black called and offered to pay Fred's way out to California to have a heart-to-heart talk with Reagan about what he could do for him in Connecticut.

Fred demurred, if only temporarily. He was well aware of what a grueling and time-consuming job it would be. He wanted to talk to his wife and consult with several very close friends. For now, it was important he play his cards close to the vest. He was still functioning as Connecticut GOP Chairman and he wasn't sure he was ready to relinquish that role.

At that time, there were seven candidates angling for the Republican nomination, including Bush, Senator Robert Dole of Kansas, former Texas Governor John Connally, Senator Howard Baker from Tennessee, Representative Phillip Crane and Representative John Anderson, both from Illinois, and several others who were toying with the idea of entering the race.

However, Bush was the acknowledged contender, which put Fred in a rather awkward position. Obviously, Fred knew George H.W. Bush well. He'd worked for his father, created the Award Dinner that still bore Prescott Bush's name, and had been gearing up as one of Bush's Connecticut campaign organizers for the 1962 election, when the Senator decided not to run again.

Fred decided there was only one way he was going to be able to truly decide who to support. He flew out to Los Angeles. Walking into Reagan's home, Fred was struck by the sight of a stunning grand piano literally covered with over one hundred photographs. He paused for a brief moment to admire it and then they got down to business.

"I want to know if you will go to work for me," Reagan stated simply. Ronald Reagan knew a good deal when he saw one. He was well aware that, in addition to being Connecticut GOP Chairman, Fred held the position of Chairman of all 50 State Chairmen. He was well liked and respected among his colleagues, so there was no doubt he could bring quite a bit of influence to bear.

The official title Reagan offered was National Chairman of Republican State Chairmen for Ronald Reagan. Fred explained that he needed some time to think about it. Strangely, finances were never discussed, although there was no doubt this would be a complex and involved job requiring the fourteen-to-eighteen hour days that were de rigueur in national political campaigns.

There was a lot to consider.

Fred had just been appointed head of Transportation for the Republican National Convention nationwide. He was Chairman of the Northeast Chairmen, Chairman of all 50 State Chairmen, and Chairman of the Republican Party of Connecticut. All of which he would have to resign if he went to work for Reagan.

It was one of those situations where there simply was no hard and fast answer. Weighing the facts and figures, debating the poll numbers and the possibilities only goes so far. In the end, it comes down to gut instinct. Something that Fred had learned to listen to long ago.

However, this time, the stakes were higher than they had ever been. As he turned the idea over and over in his mind, Fred found that he kept thinking it was Reagan's turn to be President. No reason or rationale behind the thought, but a growing conviction that he couldn't shake. The timing was right. This was going to be Reagan's great challenge.

"I had to be a part of it," Fred explained. "Violet and I talked it over, and even though I had a home and three kids to support with no idea of what kind of money I was going to make, we agreed. I was going to take the job."

Within a few days, John Sears called. He wanted to meet with Fred to hear and discuss his answer. Fred understood why Sears wanted to meet in person, but he needed to walk a fine line. He would have to deal with the political fall-out based on the multiple resignations he was about to submit, while making sure that he maintained his political capital which he would need to leverage in the very near future.

If he was seen conferring with John Sears in Connecticut, it would take away his ability to manage the process. They agreed to meet at the Jockey Club in Washington, D.C. around 5 o'clock before the early evening crowd showed up. Sears was seated at a small table in the back of the room, Fred moved to join him. There were a few people scattered around, but they were far away from their table and would not be able to overhear the conversation.

Seeking anonymity in a revolving door city like Washington is what many people do when they don't want to be seen. They place themselves in plain view, knowing of course, that nobody will spot them.

Unless, of course, you are Fred Biebel and the word coincidence has become an integral part of your personal lexicon. No sooner had John and Fred begun their conversation than the Maître d' escorted a young woman into the room and seated her two small tables away.

Fred looked at her and she looked at him. Then her eyes slid sideways to take in John, who nodded in acknowledgement. She smiled and said, "Fred, what are you two up to?"

It was the powerful Democratic Connecticut Secretary of State, Gloria Schaffer. Fred was busted. His secret mission to conspire on behalf of Ronald Reagan would be revealed before he had a chance to do it himself. The three exchanged pleasantries and that was that. Literally.

Because, giving credit where credit is due, Gloria never said a word to anyone about the fact that she had seen John and Fred together.

By the time the meeting was over, Fred Biebel had officially accepted the position of Chairman of the 50 State Chairman for Ronald Reagan. His job would be to travel across the United States to meet with every GOP State Chairmen and convince them, even the ones who were currently behind Bush, to back Ronald Reagan.

First, however, he was going to have to resign all his positions and brace himself for the tremendous heat he knew was coming his way. Before he had a chance to resign, word got out that he was going to support Reagan, prompting an irate call from Jim Baker, who had been Gerald Ford's campaign manager.

Fred Biebel with James Baker

Fred was asked to attend a meeting at the Omni Hotel with John Alsop, who was a National Committeeman for Connecticut, and Malcolm Baldridge, who was then President of Waterbury Brass Company (and who would subsequently serve as Secretary of Commerce for Reagan). They worked him over for the entire evening. Why would he consider committing Connecticut's delegates on such a risky candidate? How could he do such a thing? Bush was a native son of Connecticut. Where was his loyalty? What about his relationship with Prescott Bush? Reagan was a loser. Didn't Fred realize he was just some charismatic actor who was playing the part of a candidate? Did he know that he was making the biggest political mistake of his life?

On and on it went. They insisted that all the delegates were going with Bush (they weren't and Fred knew it, but couldn't tell them so) and Fred needed to think long and hard about what he was doing (he already had).

Fred was under tremendous pressure. These people were his good friends. Every one of them had supported him. They had raised money for him. And here he was inching out on a limb that they insisted was already cracked and about to collapse. Reagan had just lost Iowa, for Heaven's sake, what was Fred thinking?

In the middle of the emotional maelstrom, Fred had to announce that he was not merely supporting Reagan. He was resigning the Connecticut Chairmanship because he had made a commitment to John Sears that he would go to work for Reagan.

So that is what he did. In a letter dated December 18, 1979, Fred made it official.

Mr. John Sears Reagan for President Committee
9841 Airport Boulevard, Suite 1430
Los Angeles, California 90045

Dear John:

I am taking the liberty of committing to writing the following conditions of my employment as a member of the "Reagan for President Committee" as agreed by both you and I during our meeting in Washington, D. C. on November 2, 1979.

1. I agreed to resign as chairman of Connecticut Republican State Central Committee, the announcement of that resignation to take place on November 26, 1979 in Hartford, Connecticut effective December 18, 1979.

2. Resign as chairman of the Northeast State Chairmen's Association on December 7, 1979.

3. Resign as chairman of the Republican State Chairmen's advisory committee on December 18, 1979.

4. Resign as a member of the Republican National Committee, and as a member of the National Executive Committee effective December 18. 1979

5. Resign as chairman of the subcommittee on Transportation Committee on Arrangements 1980 Republican National Convention effective December 18, 1979.

All of the above have been completed as of December 18, 1979.

The following is an outline of my job description and respon-sibilities as agreed upon by both you and I.

1. Title - National Vice Chairman
National Coordinator Republican State Organizations
"Reagan for President Committee"

2. Responsibility - Planning, contact and liaison with all Republican State Chairmen and Vice Chairmen, National Committeemen, and Republican National Committee organizational leadership in Washington, D. C.

The odd combination of political savvy and over-trusting naiveté that was Fred Biebel was evident in Fred's very first official visit. He went to see Buddy Cianci, Mayor of Providence, Rhode Island. Like Nick Panuzio, Cianci had beaten the odds and had been elected the first Republican mayor since the Great Depression.

He and Fred had been friends a long time and Fred was aware that Cianci had full control of his delegates, due in no small part to his charisma and charm. Cianci was very media savvy and inspired a running gag based on his willingness to attend any function where there would be cameras--from parades and public events to weddings. The joke was that the Mayor would jump to attend the opening of an envelope. They met in the Mayor's office in Providence.

"Buddy," Fred said, "I want you to do me a favor. I want you to consider committing your delegates to Reagan."

Cianci responded that he wasn't sure he was disposed to make that agreement. He wanted to call his own choices.

After an extended discussion, Fred said, "Look, we've been friends for a long time and this is a crucial election for the country. I believe in this man with all my heart and I've given up everything to back him. That should tell you something. Let me talk with the other State Chairmen so I can show you that Reagan is the man to support. After that, all I ask is that you do me the courtesy of letting me know before you make your choice public."

Cianci hesitated.

"Buddy, it's important for me to know whether you're going to support Bush or whether you're going to go for Reagan."

"Fred, I promise you that I won't go public until I let you know first."

Fred was relieved and pleased to have Buddy's word and left Rhode Island for Illinois. A day or two later, he picked up a Sunday morning paper and read that Buddy Cianci had formally announced he was supporting John Connally for President.

No matter how long or at what level Fred operated in the world of politics, he expected the people he knew--those he called friends--to maintain their integrity and honor their word. Just as he had always done and always would do.

Cianci was forced out of office in 1984 after pleading no contest to an assault charge. He ran again and regained the mayor's office in 1991, only to be indicted for widespread corruption and sentenced to five years in federal prison.

In stark contrast to Cianci was George Bush's reaction. Fred and he had not had a chance to speak. Shortly after Fred had publicly announced that he was supporting Ronald Reagan, Bush was interviewed on a Sunday morning talk show. The interviewer asked, "What do you think of Fred Biebel, the Republican State Chairman of Connecticut, whom you have known for a long time and who just announced his support for Ronald Reagan?"

Bush's answer was simply this: "I know Fred. Fred is a professional. He is a good politician. I appreciate the fact that he is going with Reagan, even though I would have liked to have him with me. I know Fred will do the right thing. And, when the time comes, we'll be friends."

Like his father before him, George H.W. Bush understood people and politics. And he was right. When it was all over, he and Fred were still friends.

Back on the battlefront, things weren't looking very good for Reagan. Bush had soundly beaten him in the Iowa primary, an event that made national headlines just before they were to head for the all-important New Hampshire primary. In fact, going into New Hampshire, Reagan was behind Bush in the polls by nine percentage points. John Sears was not a happy man. He called Fred from the road.

"Fred, we're in trouble in New Hampshire. Will you pack a bag and go up there and see what the story is?"

Fred headed up to New Hampshire to meet with his good friend, State GOP Chairman Jerry Carmen. They had known each other throughout their political lives and had worked very closely together.

Fred Biebel and Gerald Carmen

The first order of business was for Fred to announce his intentions. Whenever a campaign was being conducted, there was a political Territorial Imperative that many politicians ignored to their detriment, but one that Fred was always careful to honor. You never went into another person's state to conduct business without first notifying both the Chairman of the state and the National Committee members. That simple piece of etiquette could make or break your candidate's chances in the state, which, in turn, could change the entire outcome of an election.

When Fred arrived at Jerry Carmen's office in Manchester, he told his secretary that he needed to see Jerry on important business. Inexplicably, Jerry kept him waiting for over two hours. By the time he finally appeared, Fred was steaming.

Carmen was uncharacteristically abrupt and demanded to know what Fred was doing in New Hampshire. Knowing that Carmen was a big Reagan man, Fred quickly replied that he was there to help.

"Jerry, I'm up here to see what I can do to support your efforts. George Bush is coming in and you've got a tough battle ahead of you."

Fred's explanation only served to further irritate the Chairman. Realizing that he had to get Jerry to neutral ground, Fred suggested they go across the street to a diner for some coffee and conversation.

Apparently, Carmen had been told that there was a problem with his state and that Fred was being sent up to see what it was. That cast him in a very negative light.

"Jerry," Fred began, "I can come into your state and we can be at loggerheads, but we've known each other too long to be enemies or to get into a fight. We've never had any disagreements between us.

"I recognize that this is your state and you're the Chairman, and I won't do anything to upset that, but we both have a job to do. I think I can help you win New Hampshire and help make both of us look good, as well as produce results for Reagan."

Mollified but still wary, Jerry agreed that they needed to work together. Fred knew what he had to do to seal the deal.

Jerry Carmen was not only a very capable politician, he was at his best when working with the press. So Fred gave Jerry his word that he would never talk to the press or even have anything to do with them – that would be Jerry's job. Fred was there to organize the campaign work across the state, which is what he did best. Their goal was to win the state for Reagan. Toward that end, they would aid and abet one another in any way they could. They shook hands on the agreement and both men remained true to their word.

There was a lot to be done and little time in which to do it. First and foremost, Fred needed a base of operations. Jerry quickly got him set up in an old, empty school building not far from the diner. Fred hit the phone. There were lots of calls to make.

The first person Fred contacted was Jack Hughes back in his hometown of Stratford. Hughes had been a political associate of Fred's for many years. He had also worked as an officer at United Technologies in Hartford and was a whiz with all things statistical.

"Jack, Fred Biebel."

"Fred, how are you? I've just been reading about you in the paper."

"Good, then you know what's going on. How would you like to come up to New Hampshire for a week and spend some time setting up polls and other campaign numbers, basically help me get organized and launched?"

"Sure."

In essence, that was the same conversation that was repeated twelve more times in conversation with colleagues from Illinois to California.

"I want you to come to New Hampshire to work for Ronald Reagan for the primary. First, I don't have any money to get you here. Second, I have no place for you to sleep when you get here, so you'll have to bring a sleeping bag because all I have is a big, empty schoolhouse." One by one, they all agreed.

Fred knew he was in for a tough fight because the woman who was organizing for Bush had been one of his protégés in Connecticut. And Helen Robbins was good. In fact, she was very good. Although they were going to have to duke it out, they both knew their friendship would survive the battle.

Fred went to work pinpointing the main cities he needed to target and sent each of the twelve people who had come to work with him to a specific city.

To get started, he rounded up ten Republican volunteers who had been trying to organize for Reagan with little success. He brought them into the school, which had a big gym floor and several surrounding offices.

Fred placed a desk in the middle of the gym floor and sat down. He then assigned each one of the volunteers their own office and handed each one a yellow pad and a pencil.

"I have just appointed each of you Chairman of the Republicans for Ronald Reagan for the State of New Hampshire. Go into your office with your pad and pencil and write down what you think is wrong with the campaign as of today. Then write what you need to change it and what equipment or facilities you need to make those changes happen."

Fred made it clear that he wanted their most thoughtful comments, ideas and suggestions. They had the entire day to do it, but that was it. By end of day, he needed those pages in his hands. Finally, papers in hand, he headed back to his hotel. There was a lot of material to evaluate and analyze.

As Fred sifted through all the pages he'd been given, one problem stood out among all the different complaints. Boiled down, the morale of the Reagan supporters statewide was nonexistent.

Nobody seemed to be guiding the ship in any specific direction. In fact, there was no leadership of any kind. There wasn't even anyone to speak with to complain about the fact that the volunteers were rudderless.

There was no equipment, there were no tools, no bumper stickers, no signs, no posters, no banners, no brochures, no pamphlets, nothing for them to pass out to people, nothing to use to initiate a conversation with voters. That meant that essentially there was nothing for them to do.

The situation was tailor-made for someone like Fred. He knew exactly what to do and he knew how little time he had to do it. Knowing that staffers would be working late and starting early, Fred called Reagan headquarters in Washington at the crack of dawn. He ran off a list of materials he wanted and he demanded that they be shipped to New Hampshire immediately. He was stunned by the response.

"Fred, we can't do that because we have a primary coming up in South Carolina and we're going to need all that stuff for South Carolina."

"Are you out of your minds or just ignorant?" he bellowed. "You won't be having any primary coming up in South Carolina if we don't win New Hampshire."

Back and forth they battled. Fred gave up trying to educate the staff about political process and insisted on speaking to John Sears. It was the only way he was going to get things handled. Ultimately, he succeeded in getting through to the campaign manager, who immediately agreed to do what was necessary.

Soon, armed with what they needed, the twelve men and women who had responded to Fred's call from around the country headed to New Hampshire's major cities. The goal was to set up operations as quickly as possible, to disseminate the materials, recruit more volunteers, make phone calls and get the word out. *Reagan for President.*

Fred ran the campaign military style. He knew he had to keep a very tight rein on what was happening where. He insisted that each Deputy report in every afternoon and describe what they had found, what they were doing, what the problems were, and how they intended to correct those problems. The best way Fred could leverage his experience and expertise now was to know what each city looked like, so he could compile and analyze the information and recommend appropriate action, then, in turn, be able to report what he had done to John Sears.

Dick Wirthlin, a close friend and associate of Reagan's, was going to be doing all of the polling. Sears had Wirthlin call Fred every night at 11 o'clock at his hotel so nobody would know they were in touch and toes wouldn't be stepped on. Discretion was important, but it was also imperative that Fred be up to date on the very latest information. That nine-point discrepancy had to go.

Other strategists had arrived and were working at top speed to reverse the polling trend. John Sears had come up from Washington and brought with him Charlie Black--now Deputy Campaign Manager--and Jim Lake, a public relations man. Lake, in turn, had recruited both of his sons to help out. There were a number of secretaries and several other associates, all of whom joined in the effort to make up for lost time.

Most of the contact with the public occurred outside and at various venues, but, on occasion, someone would wander in from the street. Fred was sitting at the desk he had plunked down in the middle of the gym floor when an elderly-looking gentleman came in moping around and looking over everything. Of course, there wasn't much to look at except a counter with some photographs and brochures.

"I asked if I could help him, but he mumbled that he was just looking around. So I gave him some literature, asking for his support for Reagan, and we had a very brief three-minute conversation and he left. I never gave him another thought."

Meanwhile, the wheels of the campaign machine were now spinning swiftly, the numbers had begun to change. All of their activity had attracted attention and there was starting to be a buzz. Well, maybe not a buzz, perhaps a quiet hum. Something was missing.

Where was the candidate himself? Why hadn't anybody thought to schedule an appearance for him? The only thing that would kick the hum into a reverberating buzz was the presence of Ronald Reagan in New Hampshire.

It was decided that the best exposure could be gained by having a debate. A debate hosted by the Republicans. In Nashua, one week before the primary. The story of the now famous, and not quite correct quote, "I paid for this microphone," is best told by the man himself, Ronald Reagan.

From the web site http://www.nhreagannetwork.com/

Reagan later recounted the incident as a "brief and seemingly small event, one lasting only a few seconds," that he said he thought, "helped take me to the White House." He continues:
"When the Nashua Telegraph offered to sponsor a debate between the two of us (Reagan & George H.W. Bush) on the Saturday evening preceding the election, we both accepted. Understandably, this brought howls from the other candidates.
In protest, one of them, Senator Bob Dole, complained to the Federal Elections Commission that by financing a debate

between only two of the seven candidates, the newspaper was making an illegal campaign contribution to the Bush and Reagan campaigns. The commission agreed with him, so my campaign offered to pay the full cost of the debate - a few thousand dollars - and they accepted. I thought it had been unfair to exclude the other candidates from the debate."

After arriving at the debate, he found two chairs - one for him and frontrunner George H.W. Bush. The other candidates were confused, as was the audience.

"I decided I should explain to the crowd what the delay was all about and started to speak. As I did, an editor of the Nashua newspaper shouted to the sound man, "Turn Mr. Reagan's microphone off." Well, I didn't like that - we were paying the freight for the debate and he was acting as if his newspaper was still sponsoring it. I turned to him, with the microphone still on, and said the first thing that came to my mind: "I am paying for this microphone, Mr. Breen." (sic) Well, for some reason my words hit the audience, whose emotions were already worked up, like a sledgehammer. The crowd roared and just went wild. I may have won the debate, the primary - and the nomination - right there.

The crowd wasn't the only thing on fire that night. In all of his years in politics, Fred Biebel had never seen anything like it. He was exhilarated beyond words. By simply being himself, Reagan had instantly become the star of the show. He was angry and he showed it. By asserting himself and demonstrating his ability to answer a challenge, he made the most Presidential of presentations. Reagan's polling numbers went through the roof.

While he was riding the crest of his new popularity, the campaign sent him on a last-minute bus tour around New Hampshire, accompanied by John Davis Lodge, the former Congressman and Governor of Connecticut and future Ambassador to Spain (and like Reagan, a former actor). The final day of the tour took place on the same day as the primary.

"I was in the hotel lobby waiting for the bus to come," Fred remembers, "and John Davis Lodge was the first to step off the bus, followed by Sears, Black, Lake, his two sons, and two secretaries.

"The press people were going crazy because this was the biggest primary of the year. There were cameras all over the place with everybody jockeying for position.

"Lodge and I moved to the hotel's small coffee shop for a short conversation. A moment or so after we were seated, Charlie Black stopped at our table and congratulated me on the job I had done in New Hampshire. Charlie added that he was on his way up to Reagan's hotel room to see 'the old man,' as he called him, for a few minutes. But, he added, when he returned, he wanted to talk with me about the campaign and how everything was going."

Five minutes later, somebody tapped Fred's shoulder. He turned around to see Charlie with what can only be described as a stricken look on his face. He asked Fred to step into the hallway so he could speak with him privately.

"Fred, do you have a car here?"

"Yeah Charlie, I rented a station wagon."

"I need it. Where is it?" he asked.

Fred told him the car was in the parking lot, covered with ice and snow. "Why do you need the car, what's going on?"

"Fred, you won't believe this. John Sears and I and the whole group just got canned. Jim Lake and everyone! Reagan just fired his whole staff. We're going! We're out of here!

"This is humiliating, devastating. I don't want the press to know, we'll be mobbed. We've got to sneak out of here as quickly as we can."

Fred not only agreed they could take the car, he went out to the parking lot and got the car going. By the time he returned, the team had packed their bags and were set to leave.

The last Fred saw of Jim Lake, he was hugging his sons. They were crying. Everybody was incredibly upset. Then he and Charlie and the two secretaries got in his station wagon and took off.

Utterly bewildered, Fred trudged through the snow back to the coffee shop. He said goodbye to John Lodge and went back into the hotel lobby.

"I thought, oh my God, I'm probably the only one in the country, other than Ronald Reagan, who knows that on primary day, even before the results have begun to come in, he fired his entire staff!

"A minute later, a guy with a little thing in his ear tapped me on the shoulder and asked if I was Fred Biebel. When I acknowledged that I was, he said 'Governor Reagan wants to see you upstairs in his room.' "

Fred knew what was coming. It was now his turn and he had just given away his rental car and had no way of getting out of town.

He went upstairs and knocked on the door. A doorman ushered him into the Reagans' hotel suite. The first thing that happened caught Fred completely off guard.

Nancy Reagan exclaimed, "We want to thank you for the wonderful job that you have done up here." Fred nodded and smiled, not sure what was coming next. He could hear Reagan concluding a phone conversation in the next room.

Reagan entered the room and said, "You and Jerry Carmen have done an outstanding job." He paused for a moment, then continued, "I want you to know that we just got rid of Charlie Black and John Sears and Jim Lake and the others."

Nancy interjected, "Charlie didn't have to go, he went because the others went. He could have stayed, but he said that if the others were being let go, he would leave, also. That didn't have to happen, but it happened."

Then Reagan turned to Fred. "Fred, we would like you to continue on with us. Now that we have changed our staff, we have a new campaign manager. He should be here in a few minutes."

"I later learned that Reagan had been talking with Holmes Tuttle, his finance man in California, who started him off in politics many years before. Tuttle had called to congratulate him because the early polls were showing that we were ahead by thirty points. From nine points down to thirty points ahead."

Within a minute or two, there was a knock on the door and in came the old man who had been shuffling around Fred's old school house headquarters.

"I had never met him formally, but in that context I finally realized who he was," said Fred.

It was William Casey, multi-millionaire tax lawyer from New York and former chairman of the Securities and Exchange Commission. Reagan's new campaign manager.

William Casey and Fred Biebel

Apparently, a month earlier, there had been rumors floating around in the press that John Sears was going to be replaced. Ostensibly, Sears had overheard a conversation in which Ed Meese told another Reagan supporter that he was going to be fired by Reagan the day after the primary. Sears was upset and felt strongly that, if he was going to be terminated, he should be the first to know about it. When nothing was said, Sears probably assumed that the now-blazing success of Reagan in New Hampshire had precluded the issue.

Later, Reagan defended his dismissal of Sears and the others before the primary vote was completed by saying that, in the event that he lost in New Hampshire, it would not appear as though he was placing the blame on his staff.

Fred had his own opinion of what had happened. In his role as Executive Director, he had witnessed an inordinate amount of infighting among the staff who, up to the point that he stepped in, had done a very slipshod job on Reagan's behalf in New Hampshire.

In retrospect, Fred realized Bill Casey had been observing the campaign for quite awhile around the country, including the operation in New Hampshire. He knew well enough what he was seeing.

There was one more surprise in store for the man who worked so fervently behind the scenes. When Ronald Reagan went on national television as the winning candidate, he publicly thanked both Jerry Carmen and Fred Biebel for their stunning success in the New Hampshire primary.

CHAPTER 2
The Dance of Power

Fred Biebel has been described as a "wily, pragmatic politician," "an astute and competent judge of the political body," a "squirrelly old rascal with ants in his pants," and a man who knew when he spotted a bit of luck, to grab it and hang on for dear life.

He is also someone for whom the phrase, "incredible coincidence" is redundant. The unlikely occurrences and concatenation of events in both his professional and personal life defy rational description. Not that he hasn't worked fiercely for everything he did and for all that he accomplished.

Fred lives, breathes, dreams and acts on his Republican values and beliefs. The man is in love with the very essence of politics. He is also willing to acknowledge that, above all else, politics is a dance.

Most of the time, it's pugilistic in nature. People in politics like that. They love the combative, deal-making, ducking in low for a quick shot then dancing away with glee, kind of interaction. The shots aren't intended to be knock-out punches and everybody knows they are going to eventually give as good as they get. The ones who don't inherently understand the give and take, the ebb and flow, end up leaving the game and going on to manage hedge funds and other more profitable pursuits.

On rare occasions, politics can be a pas de deux whereby two members of opposite teams team up to do the right thing. Ex-Presidents George Bush Sr. and Bill Clinton are a good example of what is a very rare occurrence in our society.

Most often, the business of politics is an out-of-step, two-step that expands into further discord as multiple partners enter the dance. Mostly, it is an unending jockeying for position, power and the spotlight. Not unlike the gangs of Leonard Bernstein's West Side Story, the Sharks and the Jets. Lots of posturing, not a little ritualized combat for the on-lookers, sometimes dirty tricks and, on occasion, some truly spectacular choreography that leave a single dancer alone on center stage, picked out by the lead spotlight, as the audience cheers.

Unless it's an election year, most people think of politics as the sound and video bites that pepper the evening news or cycle endlessly on the Internet. Or the bickering pundits on TV or splashed across the Op-Ed pages who hash and re-hash every local or national scandal or contretemps. There is a smaller demographic that watches C-SPAN and has a sense of some of the logistics that the business of being in the business of politics entails.

However, just as with the quintessential iceberg, most of the real substance of the beast is below the surface. We hear it referenced quixotically by accepters of all kinds of awards: theatrical, political, meritorious, etc. People offer their appreciation for the sacrifices made and claim their success is due to everyone who stood behind them. *Behind* the scenes.

What most of us don't realize is the sheer magnitude of that simple truth. Even though we've all seen documentaries that show the amazing amount of time, effort and dogged will power that go into creating things as complex as movies or Broadway shows, what goes into creating a politician's performance on any level requires every bit as much choreography and coordination.

Because let's face it, politics is theater. But it doesn't stop there. For political success, you have to add strategic vision to the mix, an infallible sense of timing, an ability to move through ever-changing loyalties and landscapes, a thick skin, an agile mind, the determination of a pit bull and the flexibility of a dancer. In Dale Carnegie's words, you have to know how to win friends and influence people.

Scale up the stakes and you ratchet up the requirements. Higher offices demand triple levels of what went before, including stamina, experience and a far flung network of people from all walks of life and both sides of the aisle.

Early in his career, in a 1979 acceptance speech to the Connecticut Republican State Central Committee, Fred said, "As I have traveled the towns and cities in Connecticut during the last few months, I have often told the story that was told to me, and I quote: 'When Republicans form a firing squad, they all stand in a circle.'"

Fred went on to leverage the rueful laughter of the group by transforming the quote into a rallying cry. He called for permanent disbandment of the circle in favor of a straight line of party loyalists, marching shoulder to shoulder toward their new objectives. Exactly the kind of motivational mantra that was needed at the time.

In that same speech, Fred disavowed the standard operating procedure of many politicians of the day by declaring that, if you wanted to find him, he wouldn't be in his office on High Street. He'd be out along Main Street and every other avenue, talking with people and finding ways to realign the party stance and presentation with their needs.

All of this would be just so much fluff and rhetoric coming from a good number of other politicians, whatever their level or party affiliation. But Fred's nature was such that he not only meant every word of it, he lived and breathed the credo for sixty years.

During Fred Biebel's career, he worked for six Republican presidents: Eisenhower, Nixon, Reagan, Ford, George H.W. Bush Sr. and George W. Bush. It isn't possible to count the number of councilmen, senators, congressmen, ambassadors, governors and committee members he has sponsored, worked for or helped.

With a career in politics that spans six decades, as of September, 2008, Fred will have attended fourteen Republican National Conventions. That is not only a love of politics, that is a deep and profound love of country.

CHAPTER 3
Evolution

Fred started working in 1942 when he was sixteen and never stopped. In high school, he would get up at the crack of dawn, work at the local grocery store stocking shelves, head off to school and then return to the store until 7 or 8 o'clock.

As soon as he graduated, Fred tried to join the military because the war was still on. At eighteen years old, he was rejected because of high blood pressure, due perhaps in part to the frenetic pace of his life even then. Hyperactivity was not a word that was in use when Fred grew up, but it certainly would describe him to a T. However, what might have been a disability for some was a trait he turned into one of his greatest assets.

From earliest childhood, he was out exploring, building and creating projects, as well as recruiting others to participate. Of course, they had to let him be in charge because he always knew how things should be done. At least he thought he did and, as time would tell, he was mostly right about that.

It just wasn't possible for him to hold still. So when he wasn't out doing something, he focused his energy on collecting things. Rocks, shells, snake skins. Later in life, that passion continued, manifesting in a range of rooms stuffed with Santa Claus characters, stamps, pipes, political memorabilia, and a huge headache for his wife.

But this was 1944 and Fred wanted to serve his country in some way. The rejection for active service was a blow, but he recovered in what would become typical Biebel fashion. Within three days, he had figured out that he could volunteer for the Army Fire Department. Thanks to his collecting bug, he still has the official badge he wore, proudly displayed next to his very first driver's license.

After attending what later became the University of Bridgeport, Fred found that he loved the world of retail. He started at Levitt's Department Store and then took a job as a General Purchasing agent at D.M. Read, located at the corner of Broad & John streets, Bridgeport, CT. No surprise there. Donna Micklus, who would later work for Fred when he was in politics in Hartford, claimed that Fred Biebel was a man who could sell the same bridge. Three times over. To the same guy.

Fred also joined The Junior Chamber of Commerce, which offered an early version of what is now called networking. But the Jaycees, as they later came to be called, were more than that. Members practiced classic leadership training skills and public speaking. They learned how to arrange meetings, coordinate functions, and organize campaigns for local and national positions within the organization itself.

Think boot camp for political gladiators. If you pushed hard to succeed on the local level, you could be well positioned for the arena of politics on the state and national level. The Jaycees not only gave Fred a taste for politics, this was where he would develop friendships that would last fifty years and more.

After his success with the Jaycees, Fred toyed with the idea of running for public office in Connecticut. Actually, he was courted by the guy who had been Republican Town Chairman of Stratford for twenty years and who was a very powerful figure within state politics. Oscar Peterson was also Senator Pro tem, a successful businessman, and very popular. Peterson made it clear he thought Fred should be his successor as Town Committee Chairman.

The Town Committee consisted of sixty citizens, six from each of Stratford's ten districts. Even if you don't know anything about politics, it's clear the math in that equation translated to non-stop battles and constant in-fighting. Things could and did get ugly. Often. Peterson had been impressed by Fred's ability to mediate and negotiate and, when that failed, to argue his point so passionately and relentlessly that others were either swayed to his side or simply gave up and gave in.

"He took me by the hand and brought me all over Connecticut," Fred explained. "He introduced me to the right people, took me to all the important legislative town committee meetings, to state central committee meetings, lunches, dinners and parties.

"Oscar let it be known to everyone that I was the heir apparent, the anointed one. He was not going to run. He was going to retire and he wanted me in charge. So I spent the better part of a year shaking hands, talking to people, studying committee agendas, researching the different factions, who was on what side and which group was trying to get what legislation passed or blocked. It was a lot of work and required a tremendous amount of preparation."

The Sunday before the official announcement and election were to take place, Fred was awakened in the morning by a call from Billy Hulton, a friend and colleague.

"Fred, you awake?"

"I am now."

"Have you read the Sunday papers yet?"

"Billy, I'm not generally psychic in my sleep."

"Well, you better get up and read it because you aren't going to believe what you see."

Perhaps not wanting to detail how bad the news was, Billy hung up.

Fred jumped out of bed and raced to grab the paper from the step. The headline read, "Peterson Dumps Biebel."

Unwittingly, Fred had stomped on the toes of Connecticut's powerful Chairman. A post office was being built and Fred's opinion on the best candidate for Postmaster was sought by several people. Fred named someone he thought would do a great job. Unbeknownst to him, Peterson had promised that honor to someone else. Biebel's guy got the job.

Retribution was swift and completely unforeseen. Peterson hadn't so much as picked up the phone to tell Fred there was a conflict.

When attacked, people generally do one of two things: they either go down in a heap or they rise up fighting. Fred was furious. In addition to being betrayed and publicly humiliated by someone he considered a friend, he'd also been completely blindsided. Once he found out what had transpired, Fred flew into action.

He got on the phone and called in the troops. When supporters and colleagues learned about the double-cross, they mounted a phone campaign and started calling every politico in town to counteract Peterson's mandate. They had mere days to pull off the coup.

The night of the election, tensions were running high. Peterson's new nominee was clearly nervous. The Town Committee had fractured along traditional lines of power and things were going to get messy. On the first ballot, the vote was thirty to thirty. They voted again. Same results. And again. And again and again and again and again. Finally, on the eighth ballot, Fred Biebel was named Chairman. By a single vote.

Peterson's treachery was, by no means, an epiphany for Biebel about the wisdom of running for any kind of elective office, on a committee or public level. He had been having his doubts about that for a while. People holding political office were subject to the often fickle will of the people. Power brokers working behind the scenes were not.

Which also explains Fred's issue with term limits. He is well aware that too much time in power can be just as troublesome as too little, albeit for different reasons. Contrary to what most people think, the only real buffer between special interest groups and a bloated bureaucracy is strong and stable leadership.

There has to be enough time to establish an understanding and build a network of people. That is the only way you can know with certitude which one at any time is going to outweigh the other. Fred's point is that, in every walk of life, the same basic rules apply. You have to get to know somebody before you trust them. To know them, you have to be able to work with them in all kinds of situations. Good and bad. Leisurely and full-panic mode. You need a good grasp of the ever-shifting lay of the land, the dynamics of different legislative groups and the needs of the people balanced in your head at all times.

As Fred puts it, "Who wants to campaign for an office that you have to run for every two years? Not only is that a lot of work, you can't get anything substantive accomplished because the minute you're elected, you have to begin your campaign to get reelected."

For Fred, the real fun and adrenalin high came from putting together those campaigns, organizing and orchestrating everyone and everything that needed to happen. It was the same as in childhood: Fred knew what needed to happen and everybody had to do it his way. One of the reasons he was so successful at what he did was because he was consistently persuasive and passionate about what he felt the right course of action should be. From helping someone make the right decision about which article of men's wear would be appropriate to choosing the best person to fill an open spot on an important committee.

In politics, on both the state and national level, people called it being "Biebelized". Any time they picked up the phone and heard Fred's voice, they knew they would either have to get out their checkbook, go to work on some committee, advance a particular cause or person, or show up at a special function. The man simply didn't take no for an answer. The notable thing about Fred's powers of persuasion is that they were never heavy-handed.

In 1964, Fred met Bill Middendorf at the National Republican Convention in San Francisco, where Middendorf was Treasurer of both the Republican National Committee and Barry Goldwater's Presidential campaign.

"Everybody instantly liked Fred," Middendorf remembers. "He was a very straight forward guy, a straight shooter. One of the most patriotic and true Americans I've ever met. So steady, such a good solid guy, you could always rely on him and he always did it with a light touch and a sense of humor."

Since both men were staunch Republicans from Connecticut, they ended up working closely together and became great friends, an association that would be mutually beneficial for many years to come. In the early days, long before Fred was first elected Chairman of the state party, he found Middendorf and Jerry Millbank were especially adept at fund-raising, largely because they were both based in Greenwich, one of the wealthiest towns in the state. For years, the three men formed a highly effective and functional team that successfully supported what was the minority party in Connecticut.

And there is that "team" word that cannot seem to escape the designation of cliché or cornball, regardless of the context in which it is used. The identification robs the term of its ability to inform situations and reveal character. People who understand the value of working in concert often succeed in situations where the "other side" holds all the cards.

Fred was a master at finding the right people for the right project. He knew how to hire and inspire teamwork and, if that didn't work, he was also capable of either raising hell or whispering so softly that everyone leaned forward to hear what was being said.

As far back as 1962, newspaper columnists were searching for adjectives to describe the intensity and tenacity of Fred when he got into a political race or fray.

In fact, he was most often involved in multiple issues simultaneously, which prompted the April 8, 1962 Sunday Herald to describe him as "the hardest worker in the elaborate" governor's race, while extolling his command of duties as the Republican Town Chairman of Stratford, having moved up from councilman of Lordship's 10th District. The article underscored his senior strategist position, noting the intriguing mystery surrounding the details of the campaign and its goals.

One interesting note that developed in complexity in the evolution of Fred Biebel as "political animal" was his ability to shapeshift. The term shapeshift appears in folklore all over the world though it is most familiar as a Native American term. It describes one who can appear to be in a particular place or of a certain shape one moment, while also appearing miles away as something quite different. Not surprisingly, the Shapeshifter can also reappear back where he started without giving the appearance that he had moved at all.

In this way throughout his career, Fred was capable of orchestrating all kinds of negotiations, gathering information, arranging sensitive meetings, enacting plans and designing events. People knew he was a diligent and dedicated worker; they just had no idea what a mastermind he was at engineering the vast understructure that supported a run for office, the passage of a bill or the creation of new committees and power bases.

A case in point is Fred's bid to help Edwin May run for Governor in 1958. Fred had what appeared to be a window-shade style roll-up map that delineated all one hundred and sixty-nine cities and towns in the state, complete with their affiliations with key contacts in other towns. When visitors entered, the map was quickly snapped out of sight.

31

The Herald article goes on to claim that,"Another deep, dark, secret in Biebel's custody is the contents of five 'black books' kept under close guard in desk drawer.

"Each book represents a county. Each includes the names of the towns in the county, the names of the 1958 gubernatorial convention, whom they support for the nomination, the names of this year's delegates and of key party officials, and the political complexion of each community."

In the beginning of his career, the late 50's and early 60's, Fred was basically running on instinct. There was no one to teach him the ropes. He just had a knack for knowing how to go about achieving his goals. Even though he was in a small state working on a local level, don't be fooled into believing that politics on the national level has the corner on suspense, drama, and intrigue. Fred never did. In big cities and small town America, he knew that we humans thrive on the thrill of the hunt, the rough and tumble of the fight.

There was something else Fred never forgot: the fact that the tenor and tone of national politics bubble up from small town sensibilities and urban realities. People are people, whether they're Republican, Democrat or Independent, from a small town on the coast of Connecticut or seeking to stage their first election in Costa Rica. Fred's years in politics included all of the above.

The fact is that Fred lived by the motto, "Treat everyone with respect and that is what will come back to you." It may sound naïve, but it wasn't really a choice. It was a genetic constraint on behavior, inspired by those who had come before him. People who had the privilege of working for him, like Jewell Duvall and Donna Micklus, cite the fact that, even after someone had treated him badly, Fred would go out of his way to help that person get appointed to a committee or to secure an ambassadorship.

Where did all of this charitable caring, deep-seated love of country and passion for politics come from? Is it possible that DNA has a psychological and spiritual component? When you look at his ancestors, you will see that they follow a through-line all the way back to the beginning of the country.

CHAPTER 4
The Spirit of Tenacity

Fred Biebel and his forebears actually span the entire life and history of this nation, going all the way back to Edward Fuller, Fred's ninth great-grandfather. He was born in England in 1575 and stepped off the Mayflower in Plymouth, Massachusetts, in 1620. Edward was one of the signers of the Mayflower Compact. From his son, Matthew Fuller, came Robert Hatch, who was Fred's third great-grandfather.

From that point on, all of Fred's predecessors were Republicans, and that was particularly true of Fred's parents. His mother, Helen, was the Assistant Registrar of voters in Stratford and his father, Fred Sr., was intensely interested in what was going on in the world and in his town, so Fred's early life was filled with the sounds and words of what being a Republican meant. It was as if he was raised under a Republican "grow light".

At the same time, regardless of political leaning, everyone in his neighborhood, his town and the schools he attended, felt and practiced a sense of patriotism. Born in 1926, just eight years after the end of "The Great War" there was a tremendous sense of community and shared destiny.

Everybody looked out for and took care of one another. Doors were never locked and kids were free to run in and out of each other's homes with abandon. Parents took care of their kids and anybody else's who happened to be in the vicinity. There was a tremendous sense of belonging and well being.

They weren't all good times, though.

"I can remember the wind blowing through our cottage so you couldn't go to sleep at night in the winter time," says Fred. "Of course, there was no central heat so there were times my father stayed awake all night watching the pilot light on the gas stove in the kitchen so it wouldn't blow out."

Helen and Fred Sr. did their best to give their son everything he needed. It wasn't until one Easter, when there was a knock at the door and a neighbor came in bearing a big basket of food, that Fred realized they were poor. Even though he was only eight years old, he had learned enough to know there was no shame in that. The people around him took great pride in themselves and in their community. After all, they were Americans, weren't they? There was no finer title to be had.

For many people in the community, going to church was an integral part of life. Religion was very much a central focus in Fred's early years and has remained so throughout his life.

"My father was Catholic and my mother was Protestant, so my sister and I were raised as Protestants. Unlike some of our neighbors, in all the years my mother and father were married, I never heard a single argument over religion."

That changed when Fred's Aunt Helen Kirner stepped into the picture. She was a staunch, you might say militant, Catholic, the type who would walk around the house spraying Holy water over everything.

"One day, when my mother was away and my Aunt was babysitting me, she saw her opportunity. She took me to the Blessed Sacrament Church and had me baptized as a Catholic. My mother didn't speak to her for six months after that. But I figure I came out ahead because I've been baptized both Catholic and Protestant, so I'm covered six ways from Sunday."

Fred lived in Bridgeport, "The Industrial Capital of Connecticut", which was at that time a medium-sized city of approximately 146,000 people. The term "industrial" belied his early surroundings. Though at least half the city's workforce was employed by industries both large and small, Fred's father worked as a chauffeur for Bridgeport Mayor William Behrens. Which explains how Fred came to own his very first suit at the age of six. The Mayor gave his father a white suit jacket, which his mother promptly cut up and made into a pair of pants and a jacket for her son.

Fred was nine when his sister, Janice Louise, was born and they moved to a new neighborhood called Black Rock. Fred's father had become a special police officer and worked for the Ritz, an upscale ballroom located on Fairfield Avenue that hosted famous bands like Glenn Miller, Tommy Dorsey and Harry James.

During the day, Fred's father drove a delivery van for Behren's Meat Market. He would come home, eat supper, put on his police uniform, and work at the Ritz until 1 o'clock, then get up at 5 o'clock in the morning and begin the whole cycle again.

"Sometimes my father would wear a tuxedo, so he was in plain clothes, but his biggest job every night was to protect the musicians from being robbed. They were paid in cash, so they would be carrying a lot of money. In those days, they would have arrived by train, ferry or bus, though many of the big bands had their own yachts that cruised into Bridgeport Harbor."

Later, when the Great Depression hit, Fred Biebel, Sr. transformed into an entrepreneur. There were no jobs to be had, but that didn't stop him. There was no way he was going to be out of work. Not ever. He had a family to take care of. His Yankee stubbornness and ingenuity were traits that his son inherited from him, times ten. Just as Fred Sr. had it passed down to him from his father.

Fred Biebel, Sr. in his Police uniform

Since times were tough and people were hungry, security was an issue. So Fred Sr. went to every store on the entire four-mile stretch of Stratford Ave. and told each owner that, for twenty-five cents, he would check and re-check their doors to make sure they were safe.

"I saw him do it on nights when there was a blizzard going on and he had to leave his warm house to go out and walk the street all night long. I can remember him putting newspaper in his shoes and putting his shoes in the oven to dry."

About a half a century earlier, another Biebel, Fred's great-grand-father, was facing his own hardships in Bridgeport. His body had been ravaged by the depredations of his service in the Civil War. Severe attacks of inflammatory rheumatism, neuralgia and malarial infection were threatening his life.

Born in 1827 at Wiesenheim, Rheinesh Bavaria, Henry Biebel had migrated to the new world, and when the call came to serve his adopted homeland, he responded immediately. Prior to the outbreak of the Civil War he had already served eight years in the state militia. Henry formally enlisted in August of 1861.

When the rebellion as it was then known broke out, Henry Biebel, Orderly First Sergeant of the Bridgeport Rifle Company, was among the first of three regiments to respond to President Lincoln's call following the attack on Fort Sumter. His Commanding Officer was Captain John Speidel.

History doesn't reveal when he was made Captain, but in that capacity, he was present at the first Battle of Bull Run. Captain Biebel then organized another company, which was mustered in as Company H, Sixth Connecticut Volunteers, in September of 1861.

In November of 1861, Captain Biebel joined the expedition to Port Royal and saw his share of action in skirmishes and battles in South Carolina, Georgia and Florida, Port Royal, Pocotaligo, James Folly and Morris Island, as well as the attack on Fort Wagner, July 18, 1863.

Captain Henry Biebel

After that, Captain Biebel's regiment was transferred to Virginia and, having participated in a series of engagements, found themselves on May 16, 1864 near Drury's Bluff. Of the men fighting in his regiment, two were killed outright in the battle, two more were missing in action and presumed dead. Forty-two men were wounded, thirteen were captured. Captain Henry Biebel was among them.

He ended up in one of the most infamous prisons of the Civil War, Libby Prison, located in Richmond, Virginia. Originally built as a warehouse for tobacco, it was made of brick and roofed with tin. The scorching summer sun turned it into a hellish environment in the summer, suffocating and dark. At night, hundreds of men lay packed in rows on the floor sweating, too tormented or exhausted to sleep. In the winter, when the average low temperatures were in the thirties, they lay side by side in the bitter cold, awaking with frost and ice so thick upon them, they couldn't scrape it off.

Lieutenant Colonel F.F Cavada, a prisoner of war at Libby Prison from 1863 - 1864 invoked a haunting image of the place: "There is something about it indicative of the grave, and, indeed, it is a sort of unnatural tomb, whose pale wan inhabitants gaze vacantly through the barrel windows on the passer-by, as if they were peering from the mysterious precincts of another world."

Finally, on March 1, 1865, Henry Biebel was exchanged and arrived home, "a physical and mental wreck," according to his 1883 obituary.

His wife and six children did their best to nurse him back to health, but he never recovered. Though he tried, he was not physically capable of any manual labor and spent much of the last thirty-two years of his life suffering in bed. Henry Biebel was in his fifty-sixth year when he died. The very last line in his obituary reads, "Politically, he was a staunch Republican all his life here."

John Spiedel, Biebel's former Commanding Officer, was called to provide an affidavit so that Henry's widow could finally be granted her meager pension of some twelve dollars a year, based on her husband's courageous service.

Here in part, is his testimony.

I, John Speidel, late Lieutenant of 6th Regt, Conn Vols, and for the last thirty years a Resident of Bridgeport, County of Fairfield and state of Connecticut, certify an Oath that I was well acquainted with Henry Biebel... That he was a well man when he entered the Service. I was not with the Regs, when he was captured but have seen him on his return from Rebel prison on or about the 16th day of March 1865, being then in a most wretched Physical Condition. He was sick for a long time and was not expected to recover. I have since seen him frequently up to the time of his death sometimes daily or weekly... with the aid of his wife and children he tried to get along the best he could... In fact he was suffering from almost all imaginable diseases... Captain Biebel had attacks of Rheumatism and Neuralgia frequently during each and every year from the time of his discharge to his death.... that the diseases from which he died were due entirely to his military service."

Captain Biebel's wife was granted her pension.

Among the many coincidences of Fred's life, perhaps one of the strangest occurred when he was at a Junior Chamber of Commerce meeting one night. After the meeting was over, all the participants went to a local bar for a drink. Fred met a young Jaycee his own age whose last name was Kosh. They got to talking, and Fred kept telling him his name seemed very familiar to him though he couldn't say why. They explored a number of possibilities whereby they might have met, but nothing rang a bell. Still, Fred's mind was worrying at it like a bone all night.

The sense of recognition was so strong that Fred decided to go through his papers when he got home. He hit pay dirt. Kosh's great-grandfather had not only served in the same Company as Captain Biebel in the Civil War, but believed Biebel was the last person he saw before he himself was captured. Another remarkable coincidence. But there is more. It was Kosh's great-great-grandfather Rudolph Kosh, who not only signed Lieutenant John Seidel's deposition as a Witness, but was also himself deposed.

He testified that he "was well and personally acquainted with the said Captain Henry Biebel for 29 years and that he served in the same company and Regiment with him from the commencement of the war."

Kosh goes on to say that they were in action together at Fort Wagner on the 18th of July, 1863 "when he knew said Captain Biebel was a well man. That he, having been captured by the enemy (himself) lost sight of said Capt Biebel until on or about the 19th day of October 1864, then saw him again, at Fort Asylum in Columbia, SC." Both men were prisoners of war.

Kosh describes what he saw. "Captain Biebel being at that time apparently a living skeleton with a few rags on his body, pieces of tent canvas tied around his feet for shoes, his eyes protruding and his limbs swelled from Rheumatism."

Terrible words describing a terrible image. The sacrifices made by Fred's great-grandfathers on behalf of this country are part of the legacy he feels in his bones and knows in his heart. All those who went before have paved the way for what we all have now.

Fred has always understood his role as a steward of the precious gift of freedom passed down to him. He has worked hard to ensure that inheritance will be preserved for the generations that follow him. An easy thing to say, but within his own family, there is direct evidence that the lessons have been taught, heard and embraced.

Fred's great-grandchildren range in age from ten years to six months and his grandchildren from thirty-five to fifteen. It isn't often you hear about a nineteen year old college student who comes home and makes a bee line to see his grandfather. "I'll come home from school and I just come over," Bruce says. "We'll just talk, see what is going on with each other."

Bruce is not only proud of what his grandfather has done, he's impressed by who he is. "I tell my friends about Grandpa and Reagan. He's done so much. He just keeps going and it inspires other people to keep going and to not give up because he never gives up. He's a big inspiration to me and to everyone he meets."

Even more remarkable is hearing a fifteen-year-old teen say to his grandfather, "Thank you for bringing the entire family up in a way that we can do anything that we put our mind to. Thank you for giving us the opportunity to follow what we want to do."

Freddie Knapp, Fred's youngest grandchild, continues, "I think Grandpa opened up opportunities for not just me, but for all our cousins, too. We've been exposed to all these amazing things, like when we went to visit the Capitol in Washington with my Mom. Plus, I've done papers at school because he got me interested in the Civil War and history."

Somewhere in time, Captain Henry Biebel must be smiling.

CHAPTER 5
The Price of Independence

Helen Biebel, (not to be confused with Aunt Helen Kirner) was an ardent Republican and as devoted to her community as her husband was. When people reference "salt of the earth" as a sociological characterization--in terms of being practical, highly capable, with an inherent sense of wisdom--they are describing Helen Biebel. She and Fred had a close relationship, although she was more of a disciplinarian than his father was. As her great-grandson, Freddie Knapp, commented, "Women run this family, they always have. Without them, nothing would work."

Fred concurs. "I have always worked well with and for women. Maybe because my mother was a strong and resourceful woman. I had tremendous respect for her. Certainly I never expected anything but the best from the people who worked for me, male or female."

One day, before her son got married, Helen and Fred took off for a week to Massachusetts to research the family genealogy. Helen's maiden name had been Hatch. Years later through the contacts he had developed, Fred was able to obtain the original documents pertaining to both sides of his family.

Fred Jr., and Helen V. Biebel

What Fred and his mother discovered about her side of the family was amazing and, not surprisingly, filled with the ever-present coincidences.

As early as 1664, and probably as far back as the time of King Edward who reigned from 1272 to 1307, the British Royal Navy would kidnap or "impress" their own people as well as enemies captured at sea to be used as crew for their warships. They needed able bodied seamen who knew how to handle the lines, climb the rigging and man the guns.

To be pressed into service by the enemy was bad enough, but to have to fight and kill one's own countrymen was far worse. The English were still "impressing" American sailors as late as 1812--in fact, it was a secondary cause of that war. Great Britain did not believe in the concept of naturalization so their explanation was, "Once an Englishman, always an Englishman."

According to his obituary in 1814, Robert Hatch--Fred's great, great-grandfather--suffered such a fate. Worse, it is likely the same thing later happened to his beloved son.

Born in Falmouth Mass, August 14, 1757, Robert Hatch went to sea at an early age. He was captured and taken on board a British Man-of-War just before the Declaration of Independence in 1776. Hatch spent three-and-a-half years fighting his own countrymen. He was severely wounded in the thigh and both legs in three separate battles. Finally, he managed to escape. "He immediately took up arms in defense of American Independence, which he supported with credit to himself and honor to his country," claim the historical papers in Fred's possession.

After American Independence had been won, Captain Hatch moved to Charleston, South Carolina, and worked for the West India Trade, though the ever present danger of pirates and patrolling British Frigates remained a constant menace.

"I have a son that has been torn from me upwards of three years and a half, and although I have sent on every necessary document to to prove his nativity, I cannot get his discharge and the last account that I had of him was that he was on board of the HMS Frolic when the action took place between her and the USS Wasp and not having heard of him since, I fear that he has fallen a victim of their arbitrary mode of manning their ships."

In fact, both the USS Wasp and the HMS Frolic sustained heavy damage during the battle on October 18, 1812. Though it appeared to be a victory for the U.S., the USS Wasp was later forced to surrender to HMS Poictiers. If Hatch's son had made it on board the American ship and was still alive, he was now most certainly back in British hands.

Though in pain as a result of his war injuries, Hatch was the sole support for his elderly mother and seven children. He had become a river pilot and sail master for the American Navy. Originally, his ship was known as Gunboat No. 166. She served to protect the coastal commerce of the Carolinas. When the War of 1812 broke out, the schooner was the first of four ships in naval history to be called the Alligator.

Though some of the details differ according to various historical accounts, including Hatch's obituary, the gist of the story remains the same. On January 29, 1814, as the Alligator was coming from St. Helena to Charleston, Hatch discovered two ships, a frigate and a brig, in pursuit of them. The Alligator put into the Stone River.

Alligator's Sailing Master Bassett said to Captain Hatch that they "had better run higher up as in all probability the boats would send a night expedition to cut her out." Captain Hatch replied, "that they cannot send their boats in without they have extraordinary pilots, but if they do come, we will dose them."

Somewhere between 7:15 and 9:00 p.m. with the Alligator tucked into the bend in the river called the Wapoo Cut, lookouts spied six or seven smaller boats approaching with muffled oars not fifty feet from the Alligator's position. The Alligator hailed the newcomers, who responded by opening fire with boat carronades and small arms.

The Alligator cut her cable and returned a fusillade of fire. But in the early part of the action, "Captain Hatch received a wound just below the temples, which took out both of his eyes. Still he could not be persuaded to go below, and remained on deck encouraging his crew exclaiming, 'Take good aim, my lads, and don't waste your ammunition,' until the battle was over. The attackers rowed out of harm's way having suffered heavy casualties. The Alligator made sail but then ran aground. She lost two men and two were wounded.

Hatch's obituary completes the tale.

"The day following, Captain Hatch was brought to town and suffered the must excruciating pain for six days, when he resigned his soul to his maker. Thus terminated the life of a brave man who was a kind and indulgent parent, a tender and affectionate husband, and a generous and benevolent neighbor and friend."

Fred experiences a tremendous sense of pride and humility each time he reviews the lives of Robert Hatch and Captain Henry Biebel. He is aware of the odd coincidence that they both died when they were fifty-six years old and he is awestruck by the degree of suffering and the extraordinary courage his ancestors were required to summon- -not once, not twice, but repeatedly throughout their lives.

CHAPTER 6
Violets Are Blue

Paradoxically, serendipity or Synchronicity as some would call it, has always been a defining factor in Fred's life. For a guy as pragmatic, logical and down to earth as he, intuition and the ability to be at the right place at precisely the right time have factored into his successes again and again. On a personal level as well as a political one.

It was a sultry summer night in late August 1950. Fred was standing inside a steamy little wooden shed selling tickets at the Fairfield University Summer Concert in Fairfield. It was the final night of the series and he was tired. Fred planned to head home at the end of his shift so he could get some sleep and be ready to go to work at his day job.

As he was getting ready to leave, a buddy who was also working at the concert popped his head in and invited Fred out for a drink. He and his girlfriend had invited one of the other girls who took tickets and guided patrons to their seats to join them. All the tickets had been sold, the customers were in their seats and the music had begun. Fred hesitated, thinking longingly of his bed, but that indefinable tuning fork within him began to vibrate and, before he knew what he was saying, he agreed to go.

1951 Engagement photograph of Violet Biebel

Her name was Violet Kline and Fred knew, the moment he saw the stunning brunette with the aquamarine-green eyes, he was going to marry her. All through the long weeks of the concert series, she had stood not twenty-five feet away, tearing in half the tickets he had just sold to concert goers. Yet their paths had never crossed. Nor would they have, had he not agreed to go that night.

Violet was not as sure about Fred. "He had to work at it a bit," she smiles. "I needed to be convinced." She shrugs, "I guess maybe I was one of the few people in his life he really had to work hard to persuade." By December, Fred had given Violet a ring and they were married the following June.

While many adjectives have been used to describe Fred Biebel over the years, romantic was never one of them. Predictably, the human whirlwind in a bottle took his new bride to a Jaycee convention in Florida for their honeymoon.

That trend continued throughout the years as most, though not all, of the family trips were based on where a political meeting, strategy session or convention was being held. When the family came along, they followed their own pursuits while Fred attended meetings and negotiations, social functions, strategy sessions, press briefings, honorary ceremonies and every other possible iteration of political duty you can imagine.

The name Violet is beautifully suited to the tall beauty whose green eyes were electrified whenever she wore any shade of the color purple. Shakespeare used the Latin form of Violet, Viola, as the name of the enterprising heroine in Twelfth Night who plays the part of both male and female with great wit and charm. Not so far from the reality of Vi having to play both mother and father to her kids, while her husband was out entertaining visiting politicos, hobnobbing with The Powers That Be and attending endless luncheons, dinners, parties and ceremonies.

Violet had her own activities and associations that took her time and attention. And when the mood struck her, she would accompany

Fred to parties and events in Hartford and later in Washington, D.C. although she was more of a homebody. Fred and Vi had a lot of mutual friends in politics but, for Violet, attending a purely political function was like going to somebody else's high school reunion. Boring at best and, when bad, there was the inevitable rubber chicken to confront.

Besides, Violet got the biggest kick out of raising her three kids; Kevin, Karen and Kyle. She was a natural at it. Which is not to say she didn't miss having her husband around and that later, Fred did not come to regret having missed so much of his kids growing up. He did his best to make up for his protracted absences by gracing his grandchildren and great-grandchildren with as much time and attention as possible. Yet, for the twenty years he commuted to Hartford, and afterward to D.C., there were times of loneliness and depression for Violet, times that without her husband she just felt blue.

As Fred himself readily concedes, planning for the future was not one of his strong suits. There were always so many projects to be involved in, so much on the horizon that he just never stopped to think about what might happen if the gravy train failed. People functioning behind the scenes don't get paid benefits, they don't participate in 401K plans or receive pensions. These days, whenever he is talking to young people, his own or others, about politics and work, Fred always stresses the need to find a way to obtain a pension and to provide for your family's future.

At one point in 1970, Fred did create a lucrative venture called Public Affairs Consulting Executives (PACE). The company did quite well for five years and then, as he ruefully admits, he chose the wrong time to sell it. As brilliant as his timing in politics was, Fred's business timing was utterly abysmal, and he is the first to admit it.

"Just to give you an example of what I'm talking about, my son came to me one day and asked me if I had $75,000.00 I would like to invest. I said yes, but what do you want me to buy, and he replied,

A gull-wing Mercedes. Within the next couple of years, that car is going to triple its value.'

"At the same time Kevin wanted me to invest in the car, I was approached by a guy who wanted me to buy some stock involving oil wells, coincidentally (there's that word again)"... also for $75,000.00.

"I bought the stock in the oil wells and never saw a penny of my $75,000.00. As for Kevin's Mercedes, it more than tripled, it *quadrupled* its value to $350,000.00. And that's the story of my life. I have been in the real estate business, the investment business, even the magazine business when I bought and then sold at the wrong time, what is now *Connecticut Magazine*.

"I could second-guess political decisions, but I couldn't second-guess the market place. I soon learned that business was not my forte--my forte was politics and people. So I may not have made it as a tycoon, but I lucked out and have a very successful family life, a good marriage, a great bunch of kids who didn't get in any trouble, great-grandkids, and now great-great-grandkids."

For all of Fred's unlucky endeavors in business, he did finally get a break and a small pension when Connecticut Governor John Rowland hired him in 1995 as Public Affairs Director and Business Director for the Connecticut State Labor Department. Fred held those positions for ten years.

However, these were still the early days and Fred was at Mach Ten at all times. Violet calls him "The Energizer Bunny" and she above anyone would be in a position to know. She affirms the fact that he only has two gears: passing gear and park. Most of the time he operates at full throttle until the needle approaches empty. At which point he redoubles his efforts in order to get *whatever* done before it's too late. He then coasts to a stop on mere fumes and will hold still only so long as it takes to fill up again.

"For someone with all his street savvy and people smarts, Fred can be kind of oblivious," she says. "He also isn't as tough a cookie as he makes out. Sometimes, he just trusts people too much. He always gives them the benefit of the doubt, and lots of times, it's backfired on him."

For all the history, civics and political education that Fred taught his kids, grandkids and great-grandkids, it was Violet who raised them. Played with them. Went to recitals and football games and teacher's conferences. Who built forts, and used her gifts as an artist to create stunningly realistic backdrops for play, copied directly from *National Geographic*. Vi raised her own kids, her grandchildren and her great-grandchildren, so their parents could also go out and function in the work world.

She doesn't understand how extraordinary her legacy to the family has been. As big as this family tree has become, Violet has been the roots and the trunk that allowed all the different branches to grow. Although with such high-powered family members functioning in the "outside" world, she doesn't appreciate the powerful foundation that her continuous, creative and loving presence created.

But her family gets it. Karen's daughter, Jennifer, says it this way, "Grandma doesn't realize what she did. She not only raised my mom, Kevin and Kyle, but she raised me and my brother and sister. Then, when my daughter was born, my husband and I were still in college. So we came to live with my Mom, but she was still working. So Grandma said, 'stay in college, don't worry about daycare, 'and she basically raised my daughter. When Kayla talks, I hear her say all the things that my grandmother taught me.'"

Karen's son, Jimmy--a veteran cop and father of two himself--remembers, "Every morning, we would get dropped off at Grandma's house before school. Mom and dad would go to work and Grandma would give us breakfast and then she would take my sister and me right down the street to Lordship School. We'd do the same ritual in reverse in the afternoon, snacks at Grandma's house and some kind of arts and crafts fun that she had devised. Lots of times, our parents had to work late, so we'd just stay at Grandma's house. We always looked forward to Friday afternoons because Gramps would be flying in from Washington to Lordship Airport for the weekend."

Violet laughingly tells about the number of times she stood at the tiny local airport and watched as the puddle jumper approached the airstrip. Standing on the tarmac, she would start to wave, knowing Fred could see her, but the plane would just keep on flying right past her, on its way to Hartford. She would heave a sigh, get in the car and drive the hour up to Hartford to retrieve her husband.

Lordship Airport was close to the salt marshes and Long Island Sound. Wisps of mist could quickly transform into fog which could just as easily dissipate as though it had never been. Whether an incoming plane could actually land at the airport was a fifty-fifty shot and, often not decided until the aircraft was in descent mode, lined up for the runway.

CHAPTER 7
Politics Makes Strange Bedfellows

Long before there were grandchildren in the picture and years before he made it to Washington, Fred was working his way up the political ladder.

In 1964, Searle Pinney became the Republican Party Chairman of Connecticut and Fred became his assistant as Executive Director of the Republican Party. The reality was that Pinney was far more interested in pitting himself against John Bailey, his legislative rival on the Democratic side, and did not want to be bothered with the nuts and bolts of day-to-day operations.

All of the political grunt work landed on Fred's shoulders, including recruiting new people, organizing whatever committees Pinney needed, running training or information seminars, etc. The work was thankless, but Fred saw it as laying a good foundation for his intended run at becoming State Chairman when the time was right. In addition to his work as Executive Director, Fred continued working with the Jaycees.

At one point, both Searle Pinney and John Bailey came to Fred and asked for his help in defeating a bill that was being brought by liquor distributors who wielded considerable clout. This was Fred's chance to prove himself and he wasn't going to blow it. It took him the entire legislative session, but in the end, Fred succeeded and the bill never saw the light of day.

John Bailey went on to become National Chairman of the Democratic Party for the longest term in history and was instrumental, along with Abe Ribicoff, in promoting John Fitzgerald Kennedy to be President of the United States. At this point in time however, he was the long-time Democratic party boss of Connecticut and he was impressed with Fred Biebel.

In the way of the times back then, both sides of the aisle would work with and for one another when they weren't engaged in pitched battles over a specific issue.

"John carried his power everywhere he went," says Biebel. "If you were walking the halls of the capitol, you'd just naturally step aside when he walked by because his cigar-smoking, glasses-tilted-up-on-his-forehead attitude said you'd best or he'd just run you down. He was actually a good man, I knew his wife and daughter very well."

John Bailey asked Fred if he would like to become Executive Director of the Liquor Industry.

"I don't know John, what's that all about?"

"Well, there is an organization called The Wine & Spirit Wholesalers of Connecticut. They're located in Stamford, Connecticut, and they have a man who is going to retire. They're looking for someone and I have a lot to say about who takes that job. How would you like it?"

"Depends. How does it work?"

"Three things you need to know. Number One, you don't have to go to Stamford, you can move the office to your home town if you want. Number Two, there's thirty-six wholesalers in the State that you would work for. Number Three, the salary is $12,000.00 a year, but it comes with a very lucrative expense account, it will cover your travel around the state."

"Let me check it out and get back to you, John."

And that is how Fred came to be a liquor lobbyist. Popular misconception has made the word "lobbyist" one best not uttered in polite society, but the reality is that governments of any size can't operate without them. Legislators are called upon to make decisions regarding hundreds of subjects, industries and issues. There isn't any possible way each senator could do the research required to understand all sides relating to each and every issue.

Though long since corrupted into an inappropriate power base that both sides of the aisle are subject to, the original idea behind lobbyists was to have every side of an issue represented by an expert who could succinctly deliver their pitch for their chosen outcome. The choice of which side was most persuasive was up to the legislators.

That was the whole idea of intermixing working with colleagues on your side of the aisle with opponents and the media. The ability to socialize and interact created more of an atmosphere of trust and cooperation. History has shown the dark side of that reciprocity is corruption and favoritism. What people often forget is that between the highs and lows on that spectrum are the working politicians who really do care and are true public servants.

Commuting to Hartford, traveling all over for the Jaycees and also functioning as Executive Director of the Liquor Association were just some of the reasons Violet rarely saw her husband. Though on at least one occasion, their rare times together proved (coincidentally) politically profitable for Fred.

"I met Doc Gunther when he and his wife, Pat, and Violet and I were at a dance at the Ritz Ballroom. We were in the middle of the floor and we bumped into each other. Naturally, we introduced ourselves."

It turns out that Doc was something called a Naturopathic Doctor, which Fred had never even heard of before. The two men and their wives became friendly and the conversation naturally turned to politics. As a fairly new resident of Stratford, Doc decided he wanted to get into politics.

Who better to introduce him to the local scene than Fred Biebel? Fred was impressed with Doc's encyclopedic knowledge. He considered him an expert on the economy, on marine life, on fishing, on sailing, in fact, anything the man turned his mind to.

Over the years, Doc built quite a reputation for himself. He was the first to declare concern for the environment decades before it became a popular subject, and particularly where the economics of Long Island Sound was concerned. He swore like a sailor and fought like a wildcat for any cause he deemed worthy.

When Fred agreed to nominate him for an opening on the Board of Education, he had no idea what he was getting himself into. Naturally, with Fred's backing, Doc was elected. That's when the fur began to fly.

"I was Town Chairman at the time," Fred says, "and Doc became a rabblerouser. He was independent and would not follow the party line. He was just an agitating guy.

"He even threatened to run against me as Chairman of the party, and, as a matter of fact, he *did* run against me, but I clobbered him."

Finally, Fred's irritation with the man who insisted on following his own ideas and beliefs and confounding Fred at every turn became intolerable.

"One day, I sat down with my executive committee and I said, 'you know, this guy is nothing but trouble. There is a vacancy in the Connecticut State Senate. Why don't we put Doc's name up for that because he can't win. He'll lose and we'll never hear from him again.' Everybody thought that was a great idea, so we did."

Surely, you can guess what happened next. Doc won handily and worked tirelessly as a State Senator for the next forty-some-odd years.

"So, our kicking him upstairs didn't do much good in terms of getting him out of our hair. Except that he turned out to be a wonderful Senator, did a lot of good for the State of Connecticut, and became a true friend of mine for 50 years.

"Now just because we were friends didn't mean we weren't in opposite camps sometimes. But Doc fought for what he believed was fair and right and I fought for my side and we both respected each other."

The Mutual Admiration Society that Fred and Doc had was built upon years of interaction, politically and socially. Though Doc is now eighty-seven and Fred eighty-two, both men are still sharp as tacks and rambunctious as ever. The minute the two get together, they start busting each other's chops with great glee.

Yet, when asked about how he feels about his one time mentor and long-time sparring partner, Gunther replies, "I consider him one of my best friends and I don't mean that facetiously. Fred and I had plenty of political disagreements and some of them were really hot, I can tell you. We would fight each other and growl, and the son of a bitch used to win more of the fights than I did. I didn't like that, you know, there's nothing better than winning, but we would always end up being friendly.

"You could rely on Fred. He would give you his word, or he'd say that he was going to back you up on something and he'd do it. If he wasn't going to back you, he'd tell you that, too. That means more to me than the guy who would slap you on the back and then screw you. Fred and I could always trust each other and that's important."

When asked about John Bailey, both men looked at one another and smiled with a similar knowing look in their eyes. "Nothing moved in the State of Connecticut when it came to the Legislature unless John Bailey blessed it," said Gunther. "He was The King. I don't give a damn if it was a minor item or major item, this man was in control. Though I have to say, even though I'm a suspicious old cuss, I never associated him with anything crooked or anything of that nature."

"Once I remember within the first few months I was in the Senate, I went into the hall and I went up to him. He's standing there with his glasses typically shoved on top of his head. He and Ella Grasso both did that, it was their trademark.

Connecticut State Senator, George "Doc" Gunther and Fred Biebel

"Anyway, I said to him, 'look I've got a bill that is coming up and I hope that I get a shot at it. He gave me two minutes to explain it to him and then said okay. I said, 'well, do you think I can get the bill passed?' He simply looked at me and said, 'you got it'. And that was that. No dialogue, no deal-making, just done."

Currently, Doc Gunther is pursuing historical and national designation for the Connecticut Air and Space Center, a museum which he founded.

A lifetime love affair with Sikorsky helicopters has resulted in some fifty or sixty people, all of whom are over sixty themselves, working to restore fifteen to twenty different aircraft, including one of the earliest models, the fifty year old S52, (military designation-Sikorsky H05S1). There are only 14 S52s left worldwide. The kicker of the story is that all of the people working on the restoration are original employees of Sikorsky.

One gentleman, who is in his eighties, married one of the "Rosie the Riveters" from his line. She is currently ninety-two and he is rebuilding the S52 by hand-making all of the replacement parts on it. Doc continues to advocate for the museum. He is relentlessly badgering Sikorsky to sell him the hangar in which they have all the aircraft stored.

They say like attracts like. Much as they would both publicly refute it, Doc Gunther and Fred Biebel are two of a kind.

CHAPTER 8
David & Goliath

After all his hard work, Fred was finally elected Chairman of the Republican Party in 1975. His aides, some of whom were new to politics, were a little confused as to whom they should direct calls and certain correspondence when Fred's name was invoked but different titles were attached.

"Okay, pay attention, " Fred explained. "I was elected chairman of the party unanimously in 1975 and that automatically put me in the position of being a member of the National Committee. The National Committee is made up of the Chairmen of each State, a female National Director and a male National Director.

"As a member of the National Committee the State Chairmen selected me to be chairman of the 'New England State Chairmen'. That means that simultaneously I hold the position of State Chairman and the Chairman of the New England State Chairmen, follow me?"

One can hardly blame them for being confused. Later on, Fred was also voted Chairman of all Fifty State Chairmen, so he was wearing a multiplicity of hats with duties and responsibilities that were both separate and overlapping. As his experience increased, so did Fred's power base, which was bound to cause competition and inevitable conflict.

Finding a way to get along with your co-workers, particularly the difficult ones, is one of those issues many people can relate to. In politics, that game becomes a three-D Chess match as the revolving door of people, issues and alliances shifts and morphs into endless combinations.

Lowell Weicker and Fred Biebel started out as friends. Then they weren't for a time. Then they were, and then they weren't.

The feud began the day that Fred asked for Senator Weicker's help on a project that would build unity and also raise funds for the party. Because he was a U.S. Senator, he wanted Weicker to set an example and become a member of the Key Man Committee, for $250. Weicker flatly refused.

The next thing that happened was a power struggle that resulted in a knock-down, drag out battle for control of the State party.

"Weicker was trying to not only run the U.S. Senate but the Republican Party in Connecticut while I was Chairman. I wouldn't tolerate any interference with my leadership. I didn't mind sharing thoughts and ideas, but I didn't like his style of dictating what I should do and not do."

Donna Micklus, Fred's Press Secretary at the time, said, "I just thought Weicker's ego was his worst enemy and there was always a high turnover among his staff, which should tell you something. He was a very smart man, a big personality, a big presence in a room."

Fred and Lowell patched up their differences and became friendly again. "I always supported him, I always voted for him, and I liked his family. He just tried to portray himself as the King and he got away with it with some people, but he didn't get away with it with me. "Because he was a big man and towered over people, he used his stature to intimidate others. He literally would look down on people. So, one day, I got a chair and stood on it and we looked eye to eye, and then he saw I wasn't somebody he could push around."

You don't have to be a psychologist to realize that Fred Biebel could be lying flat on his back and still be eye-to-eye with any man.

Another huge rift occurred when the Connecticut delegation was getting ready for the National Convention in 1976. Stewart McKinney--the late Congressman from the Fourth Congressional district--had nominated Fred to be chairman of the delegation and Lowell Weicker pitched a fit. He was furious. So Stewart offered a compromise. Biebel and Weicker would be co-chairs of the delegation. Fred said, "Sure, fine," and Lowell agreed as well. But when it came time to leave for Kansas City, Weicker boycotted the event and refused to go. That was fine with Fred. He was happy to be in charge of the delegation.

Fred's and Lowell's fights were always in the context of politics. They were friendly and worked together on special events like the Bicentennial Commission for the Thirteen Original States.

Which points up one of the profound differences between politics then and now. Fred laments the loss of cordiality between colleagues that enhanced their ability to genuinely represent the interests and needs of the people who elected them.

"You know, you can be bitter enemies and be civil with each other; you can have a difference of opinion and philosophy but, for heavens sake, there's no need for the venom and divisiveness of today's politics.

"That's what happened with Tip O'Neill and Ronald Reagan. They'd battle it out and then go out and have a cocktail or tell an Irish joke, and get over themselves. They enjoyed each other's company."

So, what happens when politicians are able to go out for a drink, or have a conversation or a meal with someone who is a bitter opponent in terms of legislation? Is there a chance they can find neutral ground, an ability to achieve compromise, or at the least to better understand one another's point of view?

"Here's what I've found," Fred asserts, "If you are on speaking terms with someone, it gives you an opportunity to sit down and discuss the issues more thoroughly and maybe come to a compromise that is good for the people you are representing. When things get so bitter or downright nasty, you don't have the ability to further that discussion because the very thought that you hate somebody so much means you won't even spend time with them. Then, nothing gets accomplished.

"I'm thinking about some of the legislation that I was involved with over the years, where I represented various issues or clients. I did find that, when I really listened to the other person's viewpoint, I sometimes realized I was off base, or that my client might even be off base a little bit. There were many, many times when I had to settle for a compromise that, in the long run, turned out better for the citizenry of the State of Connecticut.

"If I had gone bull-headed and forced my own viewpoints or my clients' viewpoints to the place where I wasn't willing to compromise, that bill may never have gotten off the ground to begin with. Because I did listen and actually *heard* what was being said, the bills not only got off the ground, they made for good legislation."

Before Weicker could throw a hissy fit and boycott the 1976 convention, Connecticut had to work out who they were going to commit their delegates to. Ronald Reagan was pitting himself against incumbent Gerald Ford for the right to take on Jimmy Carter.

Fred liked Ronald Reagan, but his gut was telling him Ford was the man and, when that tuning fork started to vibrate, it was hard for him to ignore. He needed to find out why the dang thing was twanging so hard in the first place.

Apparently, there was also a good deal of impatience on the part of the public and party members to have the Republican Chairman claim his candidate. But Fred Biebel remained silent on the subject. Of course, behind the scenes, there was tremendous activity going on, secret polls being taken, information amassed, but no one knew about it. So, on June 30, 1976, the opinion page of The Day called Biebel's declaration the previous day for Gerald R. Ford a "master stroke".

'NO,THANKS!'

Citing the fact that Connecticut was in no way a conservative Republican state, the paper claimed that that reality had appeared to lull the Reagan supporters into a false sense of complacency. They hadn't even opened a headquarters. By the time Fred announced for Ford, there wasn't time for the state moderates to get into a put-up-your-dukes tussle with the party conservatives.

Focusing on Fred's "shrewdness," the paper also noted that, while it was likely that Ford wouldn't carry the state, he'd do a darn sight better than Reagan, and other Republican candidates could "ride into office on the coattails of Gerald Ford and U.S. Sen. Lowell P. Weicker Jr."

Political chess games require finesse and far-sightedness. Fred figured the best way to help his party was to identify the strongest candidate and leverage that presence to balance the deficit of Republican representation in the General Assembly.

Fred's impact on the electorate of Connecticut was deemed to be so strong that *The New Haven Register* flew the headline referenced earlier, **"Biebel Calls Reagan Disastrous For State"** in big, bold type on their front page.

Three years later, Fred would once again get fired up about his choice for a presidential candidate and this time, he would go to even greater lengths to see him win. His candidate of choice was Ronald Reagan.

For now, Biebel's brinkmanship timing allowed him to succeed where Lowell Weicker had failed after more than a year of calling out to rally the troops. Here is where the ineffable quality of imagination wedded to determination plays such a powerful part.

Weicker's approach had been to harangue his fellow Republicans to broaden their base and "wake up before it's too late." However, the new Republican party chairman's idea was to reform, reshape and remake the very image of the Republican Party in Connecticut. The idea was met with considerable resistance and muttered mutinous comments from a number of quarters. At first. That's where the determination piece comes into play.

Certain images, icons and emblems are seen as sacrosanct among the groups that utilize them and who incorporate their likeness into the very identity of an organization. The Republican Elephant--in use since November 7, 1874--was one of these.

Originally, the image came from a political cartoon created for *Harper's Weekly* by Thomas Nast, titled "Third Term Panic". It depicted an elephant labeled "Republican" trampling and scattering all oppositional ideas, issues and scandals of the day.

Fred's idea to do away with the sacred image was met with resounding silence and resentment. No matter. He understood that the newly created psychological equation with the elephant symbol and its appearance every day and night on the news as a symbol of the trauma of Watergate was a connection that had to be severed entirely and replaced with a new symbol, a new vision. The man he hired to redesign the icon was the same commercial artist who had joined Fred when he purchased what would become Connecticut Magazine in 1974.

Having trumped Weicker's attempts to focus party and press attention on the election, Fred then added insult to injury when he announced his plans for a Ford fundraiser.

He was going to throw a soiree featuring a $100 per plate dinner for one thousand of the more flush Republican loyalists. He also offered $25 tickets to the event for hundreds of other loyal Republicans.

Each group was seated in separate but adjoining ballrooms which, according to Alan E. Schoenhaus of *The Bridgeport Post*, led to a sense of being "second class" Republicans by those in the "cheap seats". Now revealed is the quiet genius of the showmanship of Fred Biebel. Having allowed the pricey patrons their 'alone' time with the candidate and just before Gerald Ford got up to speak, the giant wall separating the two rooms slid slowly out of sight and the two areas "merged with the efficiency of lunar linkup."

The spontaneous emotion of unity invoked by the sudden commingling of all party loyalists was tremendous and had far-reaching effects for the resurgence of the party itself. On a practical note, the party had literally been saved from bankruptcy. More important, financial credibility had been regained and that meant that the Party coffers would continue to fill.

Fred and Lowell Weicker continued to spar over the years. In 1979, Weicker tried to talk Fred out of seeking re-election as Connecticut Party Chair. Of course, Fred just gave him the "Biebel eye" and, although challenged by another candidate, he easily won the race.

Moving through the space-time continuum in multiple-motion and having been named as Chairman of the Republican Committee of Connecticut, Fred felt that every moment of every day had to be leveraged to within a pico-second of its life. Commuting to the state capitol from Stratford took precious hours of time, even without the almost occluded rush hour highways that exist today. Fred needed a driver.

As ever, the right person for the job was delivered however circuitously, to Fred's door. Vi was focusing on one of her projects, which was getting the exterior of the house spruced up with a new coat of paint. Watching her balance on ladders and haul heavy paint cans inspired a family friend to suggest a friend of his for the job.

Violet was more than happy to hire Cliff Bunting. He lived close by and, though she didn't know him, back in those days, the simple fact that her friend did, was recommendation enough. Besides, he was 6'5". Even when Fred was home, his 5'10" frame wasn't much help in certain situations. In fact, Vi was taller than he was. To this day, Fred claims he doesn't understand how an average short guy with big black glasses ever convinced such a statuesque beauty to be his wife.

So Cliff helped out with all sorts of odd jobs around the house until one day Fred gave him the "Biebel eye". His head cocked slightly to the left, Fred stared at the quiet young man. Aware that he was being watched, Cliff looked up a little nervously.

"Tired of painting?"

"Well, Mr. Biebel," he replied, "I'm kind of finished actually."

"Hmm."

Cliff fidgeted.

"Want to be my driver? Take me to Hartford? Meetings and such?"

"Uh, sure. Okay."

Cliff spent the next five years driving Fred morning, noon and night back and forth to Hartford, to every lunch meeting, council dinner, speech and presentation in every corner of the state. Fred rarely went home at the end of the business day in Hartford. There were evening committees to chair, town managers and selectmen to confer with in every county, party dinners, fundraising functions to arrange and attend and often a host of other duties he took upon himself to complete because they weren't getting done fast enough or to his liking. All of which translated to a very erratic lifestyle for Cliff. He never knew when or if he would make it home each night.

However, still in his late twenties, he too was being exposed to a dazzling myriad of experiences and people he had never known existed. He was having fun and learning amazing things, but, more than once, he wondered if someone with more interest in the world of politics would have been a more suitable driver and companion. Most of the people who were working with Fred were fascinated by the entire zeitgeist of politics. Cliff found it interesting but in no way did it consume his every waking thought as it did the others.

Fred however, found Cliff to be exactly the right person. A quiet, non-intrusive presence was a natural quality of the man, no small feat for someone of his height. Fred recalls having him appear to be invisible waiting outside the office or reading quietly somewhere in a corner, but the moment Fred needed to get up and go, Cliff would just sort of magically appear.

When it was just the two of them in the car, Fred would sit in the front seat and either go through his mail or work on speeches and presentations. At that time, he would bounce ideas, phrasing and subject matter off of his otherwise quiet companion, at which point Cliff would engage him with all kinds of intelligent and insightful feedback and suggestions. Cliff may not have found politics to be a Holy Grail, but his consistency and contributions were invaluable to the man who did.

CHAPTER 9
Civility & Compromise

1976 was a busy and successful year for Fred. He wrote an editorial in which he literally kicked Ella Grasso's butt up one side of the street and down the other.

He railed about her inability to make good on her promises for no tax increases, he berated her feeble attempts at balancing the budget. Then he lambasted her for her failure to achieve full employment. Fred had worked up a head of steam and he wasn't done yet.

He scoffed at her failure to lower utility bills through industrial expansion, and lamented her inability to increase aid to cities and towns. Finally, he delineated in exquisite detail exactly what was wrong with the Governor, the Democrats in general, the party in particular, and how they were all miserably falling down on the job.

That same year, Ella Grasso granted Fred a rare honor by appointing him a member of the Bicentennial Council of the Thirteen Original States (BCTOS). Another example of how two political opponents could go at it tooth and nail and leave the vitriol behind when they walked out of the State Hall.

"Ella was a female John Bailey," says Fred. "She was a really tough, very thorough and smart politician. She was a perfect lady at

Connecticut Governor Ella T, Grasso and Fred Biebel at Bushnell Park in Hartford. One can't help noticing there's a lot of hot air between the two of them.

78

times and unbelievably crude at other times. If she got angry, that woman could curse you out like a longshoreman.

"And yet, just like the rest of the real political professionals, her word was as good as her bond. I could attack the daylights out of her on the floor, and then we'd see each other in the halls later, smile, and shake hands. We had tremendous respect for each other.

"One time I'll never forget, I had an opportunity to get financing for Connecticut from the Original Thirteen States Bicentennial Council. I took the $25,000.00 we received and bought a beautiful hot air balloon as the main attraction for our celebration. We had it tethered over in Bushnell Park in Hartford.

"Kiddingly, I tried to get Ella to climb in the basket. Kept telling her how regal and important it would make her look. But she refused, because she said she knew the minute she climbed in, I would cut the lines and she'd be gone."

"I had the same relationship with Billy O'Neill. Early on, we would get into big debates and I used to kick his butt every time. That made him crazy, so we'd be off to the races on every issue you can imagine."

Though he was Governor of Connecticut from 1980 to 1991, the late Bill O'Neill was the State Chairman of the Democratic Party when Fred was Chairman of the Republican Party.

The two of them battled, clashed, competed and locked horns on every possible issue and decision during their mutual tenures. However, that did not keep them from cooperating with one another when the occasion arose.

"There was a little trick some people used to use to get me and Billy to show up at all sorts of unnecessary functions. I'd get a call for some dinner or award something and it would be the last thing I cared about or had time for. But they would tell me that Billy was going and that sort of forced my hand. Turns out they were doing the same thing to Billy.

"So I said to him, look they are using us, so let's you and I make a deal. I'm not talking about our political stuff or anything, I'm talking about outside party activities only.

"'Any time one of us gets a call, we'll check with the other. If we want to go, okay, we will. If not they won't be able to snooker us."

And that's just what they did. In fact, both men went out of their way to make sure they would be available if the other guy had a vested interest for whatever reason in a particular appearance.

"Now, by this time, Billy had gotten very good at debating so, while we enjoyed each other's company and we were friends, we would still get on stage sometimes and battle it out. It was a way good politicians had of interacting with each other, you really did respect one another. It's sad that those times and that style of doing business are gone.

"Because it's really the constituents who lose out. Lots of legislation that should be in place isn't for the simple reason that the politicians are behaving like asses."

Fred also maintained an "open door" policy at all times. "I learned from Nixon never to have a door keeper. His guys kept him isolated. He was so out of touch it imperiled him and gave him a sense of power that was above and beyond the pale.

"I don't think he set out to be a dishonest guy, I think he was just so enamored with his own importance that he started to believe he was completely untouchable.

"He was also a foul guy. I mean, he couldn't put two sentences together without swearing. I can't help wonder what it would have been like to have seen Ella Grasso and Richard Nixon going at it. Probably would've turned the air blue."

CHAPTER 10
No Such Thing As Time & Space

Clearly, a recurring theme with Fred Biebel is that of loyalty. The concept is an easy one to toss out, to enumerate among other desirable qualities in a human being, though, in terms of Fred's life, there is a difference and it seems to have something to do with the DNA mentioned earlier. Not necessarily provable in a scientific sense, one can still make a case for the fact that there is an inherent *something*, that if nurtured and supported, can blossom into an extraordinary ability to align oneself with a commitment or course of action.

Invoking the previous metaphor of magnetic attraction and combining it with the altogether un-scientific assumption of a genetic predisposition towards loyalty, it remains a fact that who and what Fred came to be was rooted in his personality long before he ever heard of Captain Biebel or Robert Hatch. That seems to go double for the people who were attracted to work with him. All of which might, just might, explain what happened after the 1976 Kansas City Republican Convention.

Although Fred flew, Cliff drove Fred's car out to Kansas City, Missouri--loaded to the gills with materials for the convention--as did a number of other Connecticut delegates. Time and presentation were of the utmost importance because, though Gerald Ford had won more primary delegates than Ronald Reagan, he did not have enough votes to lock down the nomination.

That meant that, at the outset, both candidates had a very real shot at winning the coveted spot. Back room challenges and attempts at last minute rule changes were just some of the tactics being employed to swing delegates definitively toward the Ford or Reagan camps. It was time to beat the drums, whip up the crowds and fuel the frenzy with every possible mood changer and candidate re-arranger possible.

There were sticks and signs to wave in front of cameras, free standing placards, buttons, campaign flyers, literature, photographs, flags, bumper stickers, pins, pendants, everything and anything you can think of. Cliff made certain he was in Kansas City in plenty of time for the campaign staff to distribute all the materials to would-be celebrationists.

The Kemper Arena American Royal Center is an indoor arena that holds 19,500 people. Nobody seems to know just how many people were in the house when the convention officially opened on August 16th, but, by the time the nomination was held, everybody was aware that the sound level generated by the partisan delegates was utterly deafening.

When it came time for Connecticut to declare its votes, Fred Biebel stood up. Lowell Weicker was sulking at home. Fred had worked and fought hard for this moment, refusing to give up even a single delegate to the party conservatives. After proudly introducing Connecticut as the Nutmeg State, the Constitution State and a proud member of the Original Thirteen States, Fred announced that all 35 of Connecticut's flagged, pinned, buttoned and beribboned delegates were standing four-square behind Gerald Ford.

When all was said and done, Gerald Ford, Fred Biebel and Cliff Bunting emerged triumphant. It's hard to know who was the most exhausted, but it's a fair assumption that Fred was as least as fried as the incumbent President. Certainly, there was a lot more work ahead of Fred and he needed to rally his energy for the upcoming fight against Jimmy Carter.

As Cliff drove the weary but elated Chairman to the airport, Fred talked with Cliff about how important the days to come would be for the party and the possibility of retaining control of the White House. Cliff dropped him off several hours before his flight. Fred wanted to spend some time reviewing his notes and refining his strategies for the run-up to the election.

Eventually, his flight boarded and he worked through the trip back to New York. Arriving at LaGuardia airport, Fred doggedly followed his fellow passengers down the endless passageways to the baggage claim and called Connecticut Limo to book the hour-ride home.

While waiting for the limo, he rewrote a speech, reviewed his plans for the week and ran one last check of his schedule for the following day. Finally, the limousine arrived and Fred gratefully climbed into the back, settled himself and fell asleep. When Fred arrived at the Bridgeport Limousine depot, Vi came to retrieve him. It was just a few miles from home.

As they turned the corner into the driveway, Fred jerked forward as if he'd been hit with an electric cattle prod. His eyes bugged out and his jaw gaped. "Oh my God Fred," Vi gasped, "what's the matter?"

Fred Biebel was shocked speechless. There in his driveway was Cliff Bunting, busily washing the car so it would be ready for the next day's activities in Hartford. Fred never did ask him how he did it.

CHAPTER 11
Parallel Universes

Fred was thrilled to be a member of the Bicentennial Council of the Thirteen Original States (BCTOS). His love of history and his own deep roots reaching back in time through the development of what was the greatest nation on earth created a pride and a patriotism that he felt so very deeply it was impossible to express.

So, in 1976, when Gerald Ford extended a personal invitation for Fred to join him and his old friend, Bill Middendorf, (who was now Secretary of the Navy) aboard the U.S.S. Forrestal in New York Harbor to celebrate America's Bicentennial, Fred experienced a euphoria that, to this day, has never been surpassed. The drama and the pageantry surrounding the occasion were unprecedented.

Lest it be forgotten that Fred Biebel carries with him the official Coat of Arms for Coincidences & Concatenation of Concurrent Events, consider the following:

On October 28th, 1886, the dedication of the Statue of Liberty took place in front of thousands of spectators. During the dedication ceremony, music was played while the dignitaries landed and were seated at the base of the Statue. Midway through the program and just after a stunning salvo of guns from every ship in the harbor, music was again played before President Grover Cleveland accepted the Statue from France. The young man who had the honor of playing the drums went by the name of Waverly Hatch. He was Fred Biebel's grandfather.

Inauguration of the Statue of Liberty Enlightening the World.

ORDER OF EXERCISES,

On Bedlow's Island, Thursday, October 28th, 1886.

1. Music during the landing and seating of the assembly.
2. Signal gun.
3. Prayer by Rev. Richard S. Storrs, D.D.
4. Count Ferdinand de Lesseps, on behalf of Franco-American Union.
5. Presentation address, Hon. William M. Evarts.
6. Unveiling.
7. Salute. A salvo from all the guns in the harbor.
8. Music.
9. Acceptance of the Statue by the President.
10. Representative on behalf of the Republic of France, Le Ministre Plénipotentiaire Délegué Extraordinaire, A. Lefaivre.
11. Music.
12. Commemorative address, Hon. Chauncey M. Depew.
13. Music. Doxology.—Tune, "Old Hundred." In which the assembly is invited to join.
    Praise God, from whom all blessings flow;
    Praise Him, all creatures here below;
    Praise Him above, ye heavenly host;
    Praise Father, Son, and Holy Ghost.—*Amen.*
14. Benediction, Rt. Rev. Henry C. Potter, D.D.
    The assembly upon the Island will be dismissed with the benediction, and will re-embark upon the steamers, which will return to their piers in the city, joining with the batteries in the general salute.
15. National Salute. To be fired simultaneously from all the batteries in the harbor, ashore and afloat.
16. Illumination of the Statue, with fireworks on Bedlow's and Governor's Islands, and the Battery.

The music by Gilmore's 22d Regiment Band. P. S. GILMORE, Musical Director.

1886 Statue of Liberty Centennial Program

86

Spectacular fireworks escorted all the steamers filled with celebrants back to their various piers, where everyone in the batteries joined in the salute.

Exactly one hundred years later--October 28th 1986 -- the celebrants for the Statue's birthday were gathered as well. Music was played as the dignitaries were led to their seats at the foot of the great statue. Among those being seated was Fred Biebel, now a member of the Federal Bicentennial Committee of the Constitution of the United States.

Hundreds of boats filled the harbor, people lined the streets and those not fortunate enough to be there in person watched on TV. It was the culmination of a year-long celebration that began in New York City's Kennedy Center with a concert that included Stravinsky's "Greeting Prelude", which featured a number of variations on the "Happy Birthday" song.

As the guns saluted and the fireworks blossomed, Fred could not help looking over his shoulder to see if, in all the smoke and celebration, he could catch a glimpse of Waverly, Robert and Henry.

Statue of Liberty Program
October 28, 1986

Pre-Ceremonial Music — 77th U.S. Army Reserve Band
Fort Totten U.S.A.R. Center

Entrance of the Ceremony Principals
Welcome — David Moffitt
Superintendent
Statue of Liberty National Monument

Presentation of the Colors — Joint Armed Forces Color Guard

The Anthems — Cantor Isaac Goodfriend
"La Marseillaise"
"Star-Spangled Banner"

(Audience invited to sing along)

Invocation — Rev. Dr. Warren Ost
Director
Christian Ministry in the National Parks

Remarks — Francois Leotard
French Minister of Culture & Communications

Remarks — Armen Avedisian
Chairman
Statue of Liberty - Ellis Island Commission

Musical Interlude — Soloist Cantor Isaac Goodfriend
"This Is My Country" — Accompanied by 77th U.S. Army Reserve Band
"America"

Liberty Coin Presentation — James A. Baker III
Secretary of the Treasury

World Heritage Site Dedication & Plaque Unveiling — All Participants

Address — Don Hodel
Secretary of the Interior

Time Capsule — Don Hodel

Closing Prayer — His Eminence Archbishop Iakovos
Primate of the Greek Orthodox Church of North & South America

Retirement of the Colors — Joint Armed Forces Color Guard
Adjourn to Musical Closing

Master of Ceremonies

Herbert S. Cables, Jr.
Regional Director
National Park Service

1986 Statue of Liberty Bicentennial Program

88

CHAPTER 12
"Look out Mr. President!"

The year was 1975 and President Gerald R. Ford was coming to Connecticut for the dinner that Fred had so elegantly finessed. The event itself was historic in that the GOP raised a whopping $90,000. Not bad for a minority party in a tiny state.

As GOP state chairman, Fred was invited to ride in the presidential limousine through the streets of Hartford. Twenty years later, Fred would learn to his chagrin that, in addition to a few other outstanding events, the President found the ride memorable, based on how uncomfortably bumpy it was.

There may have been fundraisers or a cocktail party where their paths had crossed, but it wasn't until after Richard Nixon had resigned the White House in 1974 that Fred was officially introduced to Gerald Ford. Nixon wasn't quite two years into his second term when he left office.

Substantiating Fred's initial take on what happened when you ran for elective office, no sooner had Ford become President than he had to begin the campaign for his own four-year term. He only had two and a half years to raise the funds, seed committees and delegations with those friendly to his cause, and make himself a stand-out candidate as opposed to the accidental inheritor of the Office of President.

Richard M. Nixon and Fred Biebel at Campaign stop, Bridgeport Airport 1960

The all-important introduction came from Ed May, the former Congressman from the First Congressional District in Hartford. When he ran for Congress, he skated in on Eisenhower's coattails, though he only served one term. Returning to Connecticut, May became chairman of the State Republican Party from 1958 to 1962, remaining very active in politics thereafter. Ed became friends with Gerald Ford when they were together in Congress, and the two had remained friendly over the years.

In July of 1975, when Fred was elected Chairman of the Republican Party, he and Ed had a conversation and came up with a plan to elevate Ford's profile in Connecticut. They invited the President to the Greater Hartford Open golf tournament, which Ed May had begun years earlier when he was with the Jaycees. At a lunch meeting, Fred asked the President if he would be interested in attending a fundraiser for the Connecticut GOP sometime in mid-October.

When Ford accepted, Fred starting making arrangements for him to speak at the Civic Center in Hartford. They only had a couple of months to get ready so in anticipation of huge crowds, they re-did the entire floor of the Center, filling it with bleachers. Those were the $25 dollar seats. The advanced publicity produced a terrific crowd. All in all, it was a wonderfully successful night.

Things were great and getting better all the time. There was no doubt Fred's political star was on the rise. He had been asked to become one of twelve floor leaders for Ford at the National GOP Convention. The plan was for him to meet Ford's reelection team in Washington and get briefed on exactly what they needed him to do.

President Ford had graciously made arrangements for Fred to fly back to Washington with him that night on board Air Force One. A major airport was required to handle the formidable Boeing 707, which meant they would travel out of Bradley International Airport in Windsor Locks after dinner.

Following the rousing triumph at the Civic Center, President Gerald Ford, Congressman Stewart McKinney, and State Party Chairman Fred Biebel climbed into the President's six-thousand-pound Lincoln limousine for the brief ride to the airport.

Fred was in the middle of the back seat, with the President seated to his right and McKinney on his left. The privacy window between the front and back seats was rolled up so that their conversation could not be overheard by the driver and Secret Service man in the front seats.

The driver eased the limo out of the Civic Center arena and headed down a side street, on his way to I-95 for the twenty-minute trip to Bradley.

Even the most seasoned politicians have a reaction to riding in the Presidential limousine, seated next to the most powerful man in the world. Fred was in hog heaven, to put it mildly. This was not merely a ride, it was a full-on Presidential motorcade cruising through the capital of his state.

Directly in front of the limousine was a series of official vehicles, including other government cars; and in front of them were the

Gerald R. Ford and Fred Biebel discussing the re-election campaign

Connecticut State Police vehicles who, in turn, followed a wedge of Hartford motorcycle cops.

Behind the Presidential limo was a chase car filled with Secret Service personnel, and behind the Secret Service was a press car filled with reporters. Following them was an entire series of staff cars for the rest of the President's entourage. Flags flying, the President's motorcade made its way through the city of Hartford.

While his demeanor remained calm and professional, Frederick K. Biebel was ecstatic. His hunch to support Ford had paid off in ways he could never have imagined. He was on his way to board Air Force One with his good friend, Stew McKinney, and the President of the United States, having just pulled off an incredible political bash with record-breaking numbers.

The men were discussing the events of the night when something flashed in Fred's peripheral vision. What he saw made his heart stop. There was a car hurtling down a side street, headed right for them. It was moving at a high rate of speed with no indication of slowing down. They were going to be T-boned.

92

"I'll never forget it," Fred says. "Sometimes when an accident happens, everything goes into slow motion. This was the complete reverse. Everything happened at hyper-speed."

Fred only had time to yell, "Look out, Mr. President!" and, with that, they were hit. Without realizing it, Fred instinctively threw his hand up to protect himself. The terrific impact of the car crashing into the limo threw all three men to the floor. Stewart McKinney hit first, with the President landing next to and partially on top of him. Fred landed smack dab on top of the President.

Uninjured, Stewart McKinney struggled to get up, but he was blocked by President Ford, who was still pinned beneath Fred. As Fred attempted to get to his knees, he realized from the sharp pain in his wrist that he had broken it.

The speeding car had hit the limo in such a manner that, at the time of impact, the President had turned sideways in his fall, and the driver of the other car--a nineteen-year-old kid, actually--was facing the limo window. Their faces were within just a couple of feet of one another.

"President Ford got up and I could see the kid looking at us. Then his eyes went wild and it was clear he realized he had just rammed the President's limousine."

Gerald Ford locked eyes with the boy and saw the terror on his face. He immediately tried to get out of the car to make sure the kid was okay. In fact, all three of the men headed out of the limo. Or tried to.

Barely a month earlier--on September 5, 1975--Squeaky Fromme had attempted to take the President's life. A mere three weeks after that, Sara Jane Moore had pointed a pistol at his head. Not knowing whether another assassination attempt was underway, the Secret Service had leapt out of their chase vehicle, guns drawn. They had slammed their bodies against the doors and put their hands over the top of the car so that nobody could get in or out.

"They wouldn't let us get out," Fred recalls, "and I heard them hollering to the driver as one of them pounded on the roof yelling, 'Go! Go! Go!' The cars in front of the limousine took off at top

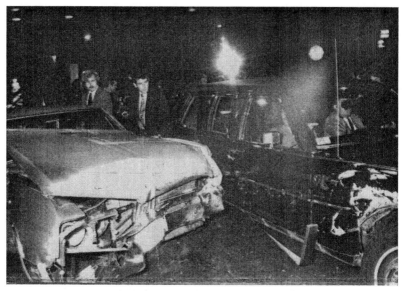

Gerald Ford's Presidential Limosine collision in Hartford, CT

speed. Then the limo started to take off, but the front fender had been bent and was pressing hard on the tire. There was no way the car could accelerate quickly."

Unaware that the Lincoln had been damaged, the Secret Service jumped back into their chase car, hit the gas and immediately rear-ended the limo. Everyone was knocked to the floor. Again.

Once everyone had recovered their seats for the second time, the limo limped slowly to the airport.

"The first thing I remember," said Fred, "was that the President's physician was right there as we pulled up next to Air Force One sitting on the tarmac."

After first checking to make certain the President was unhurt, the doctor asked whether Fred or Stewart had any whiplash injuries. Fred told him he had injured his hand.

"Eddie Leonard, who was head of the Connecticut State Police, immediately offered to take me to a hospital. But the President said, 'No, Fred's coming to Washington with us. The doctor will look at his hand on the airplane.'

94

"With that, the three of us got on the plane and I can remember Ford saying, 'Fred, I'm going to have a double scotch, how about you?' And so we had a drink on the plane and flew into Andrews Air Force Base."

By the time they arrived at Andrews, there was considerably more commotion than there had been at Bradley. Word spread quickly that the President had been in an accident and every type of emergency vehicle imaginable had responded.

Violet first heard about the incident on the radio. At that point, nobody knew if it had been yet another attempt on the President's life. There was nothing she could do, no one she could contact to find out what had happened and where Fred was. With her heart pounding and her anxiety mounting, she stationed herself between the phone and the television and waited.

Back at Andrews Air Force Base, Fred was eventually taken to the infirmary, where the doctors examined his hand, set the broken bone, put his arm in a sling and sent him on his way. Stew McKinney had left his car at Andrews, so he waited until Fred was taken care of, then delivered him to the Hay Adams Hotel, located directly across from the White House.

Finally, Fred had a chance to call Violet and tell her what happened. By that time, she at least knew that it had been only an accident, although the stories of what happened and how it happened changed on the quarter hour and for weeks after that.

The reality was that, instead of stopping traffic by posting a police officer on the corner of every side street that intersected the limo's route, the motorcycle police from Hartford were doing what is called a hop-skip. They would go up to one street to stop traffic, skip the next and then continue that pattern the whole way.

So even though the young driver was speeding, he had a green light and the right of way. He had no way of seeing the police escort going down Talcott Street as he was approaching. Which is why, as

Fred Biebel with cast after Presidential Limosine accident

Fred noted at the time, it wasn't a question of slowing down. The two vehicles entered the same space from different angles at exactly the same moment. The fact that the 1968 Buick LeSabre could even budge, let alone rock a security-modified Lincoln, underscores how fast both cars had been traveling.

What happened next was a classic government reaction to an embarrassing situation. As Fred describes it, "At about seven the next morning, the telephone rang, waking me. The caller introduced himself as Secret Service and asked if he could come up to the room to talk with me.

"When I told him I hadn't gotten up yet, he said, 'Well, if you look out your window, you'll see the place is mobbed by reporters and cameramen. They're waiting to interview you about what happened last night and we'd like to talk to you first.'"

Fred was pretty sure he knew what was coming. Just as he finished dressing, there was a knock on the door.

The agent was all business. "Mr. Biebel, about the accident last night. They're going to question you about the second accident. The thing is, we're denying that there was a second accident and we would appreciate it if you would not discuss something that did not happen."

Fred assured the agent he would not reveal anything, even though he was almost certain that at least one reporter had witnessed it. He was right.

When he went down to speak with the press, they immediately peppered him with questions about if and why the Secret Service rammed the back of the Presidential Limo. Was it a move designed to knock possible attackers away from the car? Were they told they were going to be hit again? Was it a screw up?

Fred replied that he didn't recall a second incident. There was a lot of activity with people and cars moving around, the State Police were handling the accident scene and perhaps people were just confused about the entire thing. Fred never did tell anybody about what really happened until it finally came out in the press some time later.

October 14, 1975 had been quite a day for Fred Biebel, but there was one more unforeseen consequence as a result of the events of that night.

Fred had been advised to see his own orthopedic surgeon when he returned home. Fortunately, he did so and found that the doctors at Andrews Air Force Base had set his hand incorrectly. He had to have it re-broken, re-set and sealed in a cast. Of course, he got Gerald Ford to sign it and, mad collector that he is, the cast still occupies a place of honor in his study.

Later, Fred heard through contacts that the young driver of the car and his mother's LeSabre were billed as an attraction at a Hartford car show and had even appeared on the television show *What's My Line?*

He wasn't the only one trying to make a buck on the debacle. Fred went absolutely ballistic when the Hartford City Manager sent the Republican Party a bill for $50,000 to pay for local police overtime wages in conjunction with the Presidential visit.

He sent the bill back with a note saying, "How much would you have charged us if you had actually *succeeded* in protecting the President while he was in Hartford?"

From there, the tiff turned ugly as it made the newspapers and became an all out battle between Fred and the City Manager. At that point, the Mayor of Hartford stepped in. He was mortified that the city had sent a bill for the protection of the President after the President's limousine got hit because the city police had screwed up.

The battle lines shifted as the Mayor and City Manager went at one another through the press. Fred just sat back and let them go at it. In the end, the bill was not paid and the slate was wiped clean.

Fred was surprised by the number of calls and letters he received from people everywhere, including some of the overseas Republican groups who had read about the accident in the press.

His memory of the photo that appeared in *Time Magazine* was of the limo door partially open and the President trying to get out. The picture only showed the President and Fred's leg, but word got out: Fred Biebel, always in the center of the action, but never identifiable as the man behind the scenes.

The perfect denouement of the entire event came two decades later in 1996. At the GOP convention in San Diego, the Republican Governors Association hosted a breakfast to which Fred had been invited. A number of U.S. Congressman and Senators, including Bob Dole, were present, along with former President Jerry Ford, who was scheduled to be the principal speaker.

Ford entered the room, made his way forward and sat at the table next to Fred's, with just enough time available for them to exchange a few words.

Later, during Ford's speech, he began introducing some of the people who were in the room, recognizing his old compatriots like Bob Dole, among others.

Fred continues the story: "Then he turned and pointed to me and told the audience, 'Incidentally, my old friend, Fred Biebel, is sitting right up here in front. Fred and I go back 20 years to that famous automobile ride we had in Connecticut. That's when Fred broke his hand and I had the misfortune of getting thrown on the floor with Fred on top of me. I've never ridden with him since, and I don't intend to.'"

CHAPTER 13
Honoring & Mentoring

Even though Ford wouldn't get into a vehicle with Fred Biebel, he would revisit his state whenever he was invited. In 1977, Fred staged the very first Prescott Bush Award Dinner in Hartford, featuring President Gerald Ford as the keynote speaker.

Fred had been working feverishly in the years following the shattering events of Watergate to rebuild the image and the morale of the Republican Party. In addition to changing the party logo, he had insisted they change the party headquarters address from the unfortunately named Asylum Street to High Street. The building was located on the corner of both streets, all Fred had to do was convince the Postmaster to allow him to make the change. How could he recruit a staff and new people to the party with an invitation to become what he knew people would call *Members of the Asylum*.

Having succeeded in that endeavor, Fred moved the operations from the second floor down to the ground floor where the public could easily drop in. Added benefits were the huge, one-way glass windows that allowed in lots of light.

There was one problem. The previous tenant had left a huge sign on the outside of the building. Discreet inquiries revealed that it was worth almost ten thousand dollars. Never one to shrink from a challenge, Fred called the President of British Airways directly. The airline president was "Biebelized" in short order and offered to legally donate the sign to the Republican Party.

Connecticut Republicans Headquarters at the corner of High and Asylum in Hartford

Fred knew that the best way to simultaneously build morale and fundraise was to create an annual award dinner of some kind. As soon as the idea came to him, his intuition told him exactly who the dinner should be named for.

Fred first met Prescott Bush after he had been elected to fill the term of U.S. Senator Brien McMahon, who had died in office in 1952. If you picked up the phone and called Central Casting, then asked for the pluperfect visual of a Senator, they would have sent you Prescott Bush. He was tall, dignified and handsome.

In 1956, Senator Bush successfully ran for re-election. During that year, Fred was Chairman of the 10th District Republican Town Committee and he had worked hard for the Senator's victory. Two years later, Fred was elected Chairman of the Stratford Republican Party, which gave him the opportunity in 1961 to invite Senator Bush to be the guest speaker for their annual celebration dinner of President Lincoln's birthday.

U.S. Senator Prescot Bush, Fred Biebel and Ambassador William Middendorf

"It was a small local event," said Fred, "but Prescott Bush electrified the one hundred and fifty guests with an incredibly eloquent speech."

There was a second reason that day became fixed in Fred's memory. He had been tapped as Stratford's campaign manager for Bush's run the following year. After the dinner, Fred and Charlie Keats--who had been Secretary of State for Connecticut from 1953 to 1955 and was now acting as Bush's press secretary--had been strategizing for the campaign. Both men were shocked when Bush chose that occasion to publicly announce that he would not be seeking re-election after serving ten years as Senator.

When he sat down with his team at the Old Bond Hotel, he explained that he had been having problems with his hearing. At that time, the technology for hearing aids was primitive. The Senator knew his increasing deafness would present a problem, which greatly influenced his decision not to run. He went back to the world of Wall Street banking and died in 1972.

The original concept for the annual Prescott Bush Dinner was to honor someone Fred considered a great public servant who had served his state and nation with dignity and honor. That helped define the criteria for who would be chosen to be honored at each dinner. The individual would have to be someone who had distinguished himself or herself as an outstanding leader for the Republican Party. The first dinner in 1977 was a resounding success with over five hundred people in attendance.

Over the years, it has grown in prestige and size. Nowadays, upwards of fifteen hundred people pay up to a thousand dollars a plate to attend. Not only did Fred become an honoree himself in 1990, but the Party also established an additional award to be presented at the dinner each year; The Frederick K. Biebel Lifetime Achievement Award. The first recipient of the Prescott Bush Award was Jeremiah Millbank of Greenwich, Connecticut.

Among the speakers who have subsequently appeared at the annual fundraiser are: President George W. Bush, Elizabeth Dole, Vice President Dick Cheney, Senator John McCain, Homeland Security Director Tom Ridge, Congressman Jack Kemp, Mayor Rudolph Giuliani, Florida Governor Jeb Bush, Senator Fred Thompson, Governor George Pataki, Governor Mitt Romney, Donald Evans, Presidential Assistant Karl Rove, and Barbara Harrison, Republican National Committee Co-Chairman.

Gerald Ford presenting the first Prescott Bush Award to Jeremiah Millbank. Behind them is Bucky Bush and Fred Biebel.

Lots of politicians work from the top down, which is to say that they are more than willing to go out of their way for people who are in a position to further their own cause. Like all good politicians, Fred did his share of working his contacts, but unlike many of his colleagues, he also went above and beyond for the people at the bottom--or what is euphemistically called, "the little guy."

If you were incredibly good at whatever it was you did or if you were willing to learn, if you were loyal, if you loved challenges and you were an avowed non-clock-watcher, Fred Biebel was your dream mentor. The man could see potential in people they didn't know they had and he was extremely adept at putting them into situations where it could be demonstrated.

Mentioned earlier, Donna Micklus was a beneficiary of Fred's largess. She was fresh out of college and still "wet behind the ears" when she went to work for Fred when he was Republican Chairman in Hartford. She remembers him as a stern taskmaster who was easily frustrated by incompetence or mistakes. Remember, this is the man who gave people jobs, then took them back and did them himself if they weren't doing it right or getting it done fast enough.

That said, Fred went out of his way to include everybody in whatever was going on.

"Back then," says Micklus, "the State Central Committee and the Town Chairman were the most forgotten guys in the world. Fred would take three people to a function in New York, then another three to a function in D.C. It was absolutely thrilling for them.

"He made them feel so involved and important, like membership on the State Central Committee mattered again, and, as a result, they worked hard for him."

With Fred's encouragement and support, Donna went from making hotel reservations and filing papers to functioning as Fred's press secretary. She had become highly proficient at dealing with multiple issues, managing press interactions in every venue, as well as anticipating problems and possibilities, most of which she had learned by watching him in action.

When Fred eventually left for Washington in 1979, she was utterly crushed. Her whole life had come to revolve around the world of politics. She had studied and learned everything that Fred had taught her about history and the importance of being involved.

Eventually, she went on to work for the U.S. Department of Commerce in Hartford under Malcolm Baldridge, who was Reagan's Secretary of Commerce. Jo McKenzie, a great friend and ally of Fred's, had taken over for him as Republican Chair and helped get Donna in the door.

It has been a while since the ubiquitous coincidence file was invoked. So here is one involving Donna and Fred.

When she left the Commerce Department in 1991, Donna went to work as Vice President for the Connecticut World Trade Association, which involved a New York City developer who was going to build a World Trade Center in Hartford. At that time, there were a lot of people within the organization who were displeased with the current president's leadership. Donna introduced the concept of Fred Biebel taking over as president and he just happened to be in need of a new project. Both of them were thrilled to be working together again.

Jerry Lindsley, who went on to found the Center for Research and Public Policy (CRPP)--a well known national public policy, social research and consulting firm--was another stand out recipient of Fred's mentorship. When Fred was State Chairman, Jerry, still in his teens, served as his Republican State Youth Coordinator. Fred gave him the opportunity to head the State's Youth for President Ford effort, making Jerry an alternate delegate and guaranteeing him participation in the 1976 Kansas City convention.

Later, Fred supported Jerry in being named Executive Director of the College Republican National Committee. In that capacity, he traveled to all fifty states, as well as Egypt, Israel and Communist Russia.

In a letter to Fred, Jerry cited the fact that he was proud of being called "a Reactionary Rabid Warhawk" on the front page of TASS (the official Soviet Newspaper) the morning after his condemnation of the Soviet Union on behalf of the Coalition For Peace Through Strength.

In his own words, Jerry says, "In fact, had I not met you, my life would have been very different - different career, different wife, kids, home goals and accomplishments. I owe you a bunch."

One day, Fred got a call from a gentleman who introduced himself as Dr. Luntz from West Hartford. He said, "Mr. Biebel, I have a young son who is interested in politics. I would like to have him become an intern at the Republican Party and I would like to have him work with you."

Fred replied, "I appreciate that, sir, but we don't have sufficient funds to hire anybody."

"Mr. Biebel, I am not asking him to be paid, I'll take care of that. I want him to learn how things work, I want him to be an intern in your office."

Fred decided that, at that price, he couldn't argue, so in the door walked a sixteen year old kid named Frank. Fred was immediately struck by the teen's intelligence. Frank was very perceptive and quick-witted and he and Fred had a great relationship over the years.

Frank Luntz went on to develop a new spin on the technology and application of determining accurate, real-time reactions of focus groups. At Fred's request, Luntz spoke to the Connecticut delegation before the 2000 convention.

Fred gets a kick out of watching Luntz when he appears on Fox News as a highly successful corporate and political consultant and pollster.

Kids and grandkids also figure into the equation of mentoring and success. Fred's daughter, Karen, observed first-hand how hard work and a strong sense of self could take you any where you wanted to go. As a senior manager in the corporate world--long before the glass ceiling had even been bumped, never mind cracked--she had

138 men reporting to her. She also continued the family business of politics by becoming Treasurer of the Stratford Republican Town Committee. Her sister, Kyle, mother of Bruce and Freddie, was no less confident as CFO of a large building supply company.

But perhaps the most direct "replica" of Fred's mentoring turned out to be his granddaughter, Jennifer. She was determined to carry on in Fred's footsteps and enter politics.

Then she realized she couldn't do it. "I think I knew I needed a career that I could retire with, and be able to pass down to my kids," she said reluctantly. "I saw my grandparents struggling financially when I was still in college and I think that is what made me change direction. I still wanted to be just like Grandpa, and I still want to be just like him, but I didn't want to take that same political path and leave myself vulnerable when I got older."

The paradox is that Jennifer actually recreated the same job that Fred had, only she has benefits and a retirement package. She is Director of Alumni at The University of New Haven, Connecticut. It is a non-profit organization and she is responsible for putting on huge events as fundraisers.

She does all the work while remaining behind the scenes. "I was at Ikea yesterday," she begins, "and I bought 250 vases. No one at the store wanted to help me so I wrapped each one, put them in my car and brought them back to my office. We are staging a huge event in two months to honor the head coach of the Miami Dolphins. I'm arranging press conferences and media, ordering chairs, organizing the agenda and trying to raise $500,000.00 for the event.

"When it is over," she smiles wearily, "the attendees will tell the President of the University that it's the best event they ever saw. There will be press coverage on all the news stations, and no one will have any idea that it took me six months to plan that single event." And that is exactly how it played out. Sound familiar?

There was another person who ended up being "mentored" by Fred Biebel, even though he had served as a four-star general, Chief of

Staff for two presidents, and had been the de facto Commander of the U.S. and NATO forces in Europe.

This illustration features coincidences^2. For the non-mathematicians among us, that works out to be times eight because 'coincidences' is plural to begin with.

Fred Biebel just happened to be at the Republican headquarters in Washington when he got a phone call from Ralph Capecelatro. Ralph was the new Chairman of the Connecticut GOP party and was overseeing the process of assembling a list of state delegates who would support Ronald Reagan for the 1980 nomination. But there was a problem. It was a split delegation, with one group pushing hard for Reagan and the other coming out for George Bush with everything they had.

Usually, the National Committee of a state has to authorize the slate of delegates that have been selected. Just before that process was to take place in 1980, one of the Reagan delegates had died, leaving an open spot.

"Fred, hi, it's Ralph Capecelatro. I need a replacement delegate immediately, somebody with a really high profile and whose loyalty we can trust."

"Ralph, you've got John Lodge, he's a high-profile delegate. What's the problem?"

"I'm not sure, Fred. This race is close. I need another big name. And it's got to be somebody who will stick with Reagan. Who can you suggest?"

Fred sat in silence and wracked his brain. He scanned every name, every committee, every event he'd been to in Connecticut. He couldn't think of a single person who was famous and had the qualifications to be a delegate.

"Ralph, I'm sorry. I can't think of..." Fred's voice trailed off.

When the phone rang, he had been reading the *Hartford Courant* that had been delivered to his Washington office. His eyes fell on an article that said retired Army General Alexander Haig had just been named President of United Technologies Corporation and was in the process of buying a house in Farmington, Connecticut.

"It struck me like a bolt of lightning," remembers Fred. "I thought, Good Lord! Here is a guy who is known world wide and he's going to be living in Connecticut. He'd be perfect."

"What about Alexander Haig?" Fred asked.

"You're kidding. Do you think he would?" came the astounded reply.

"Only one way to find out."

Fred told Ralph he would let him know. He picked up the phone and called United Technologies. He told the receptionist who he was and asked to speak with General Haig. When she asked the reason for his call, Fred replied that it was personal, but that it might have a lot to do with his future.

Alexander Haig with Fred Biebel

Fifteen minutes later a man named Woody Goldberg was on the line, identifying himself as Haig's assistant, as well as a fellow retired Army officer. Woody may have been a military man, but he was about to be "Biebelized," and he would never even know what hit him.

Fred explained that he wanted to put the General in the national spotlight, that United Technologies could benefit hugely from having the corporation's CEO as a convention delegate for the future President of the United States. He added that it would really be best if he spoke directly with the General because this phone call could mean a lot to his future career in politics and there were serious time constraints. In effect, the clock was ticking.

The next thing Fred knew, Al Haig was on the phone, greeting him as though they were old friends. Fred cut straight to the chase.

"General, how would you like to be a delegate to the National Republican Convention?"

"Fred, I haven't moved yet. I'm not even registered as a voter."

That, Fred assured him, was his job. To take care of the details. All he needed to know was would the General be willing?

Naturally, Haig said he needed to think about it, but time was the one thing Fred did not have. He began to weave the Biebel spell, explaining the future possibilities as he delineated the time parameters. He knew the General was a man of action. He needed confirmation faxed to him by five o'clock so it could be certified by the National Committee. It was a deadline over which he had no control.

Haig finally agreed, at which point Fred offered to call the registrar in Farmington and have her stop at his office so he could officially register. Haig declined, saying he would go to her. That gave Fred pause. He needed Haig to follow through on this, so he pushed back.

"General, you have to do this right away, sir, because I'm going to call that office to tell them to expect you, and they will call me back to verify that you've signed up. After that, I'll call the Republican State Chairman and get you put on the list by the end of the day."

Alexander Haig recognized a man of action when he heard him and was true to his word and the deadline. By 5 o'clock that afternoon, everything was handled.

And that is how Alexander Haig became not only an official delegate, but the man to offer the seconding speech for Ronald Reagan's nomination in 1980. A speech that did not go unnoticed.

Just as Fred had predicted, that first step of becoming a delegate ultimately led to higher posts. Reagan appointed Haig to serve as the country's fifty-ninth Secretary of State from January 1981 to July 1982. Which, in turn, led to the infamous incident where General Alexander Haig attempted to stage a coup and take over the U.S. government.

There are many times when politicians misspeak and they often pay the price for it. In this instance, the reporters were the ones who got it wrong, at least in terms of intent. Which doesn't necessarily mitigate the fact that the Secretary of State didn't know the correct line of succession should something happen to the President.

The assassination attempt by John Hinckley on March 30, 1981, had very nearly succeeded. The entire country was in shock and experiencing flashbacks of 1963 and JFK. No one yet knew whether the President was going to live or die and the Vice President was in the air over Texas.

In Haig's defense, as Chief of Staff, he had been credited with keeping the government running through the trauma of Watergate while Nixon's attention was elsewhere. He knew how to keep a cool head and, since the Vice President was on board Air Force Two, Haig was attempting to reassure reporters and to send a message to foreign leaders that all was well.

What he said was, "Constitutionally, gentlemen, you have the President, the Vice President and the Secretary of State in that order, and should the President decide he wants to transfer the helm to the Vice President, he will do so. He has not done that. As of now, I am in control here, in the White House, pending return of the Vice President and in close touch with him. If something came up, I would check with him, of course."

The press had a field day with the gaffe. The actual order for succession of the President of the United States is:

1) Vice President

2) Speaker of the House of Representatives

3) President Pro Tempore of the Senate

4) Secretary of State

5) Secretary of the Treasury

6) Secretary of Defense

7) Attorney General (aka: Secretary of Justice)

8) Secretary of the Interior

9) Secretary of Agriculture

10) Secretary of Commerce

11) Secretary of Labor

12) Secretary of Health and Human Services

13) Secretary of Housing and Urban Development

14) Secretary of Transportation

15) Secretary of Energy

16) Secretary of Education

17) Secretary of Veteran Affairs

18) Secretary of Homeland Security

CHAPTER 14
The New Hampshire Prize-Election & Inaugural

Jewell Duvall was a divorced mother of two, looking for a job to support her family. A friend of hers had gotten her a job as the assistant to the Public Relations Director of the Bicentennial Council of the Thirteen Original States (BCTOS) in Olde Town, Alexandria. To commemorate the bicentennial, there would be all kinds of celebrations, including historical re-enactments like the Siege of Savannah, the Landing of Comte de Rochambeau with his French troops in Newport, Rhode Island, and The Victory at Yorktown.

In Jewell's description of the Council, she notes that "There were two trustees from each of the 13 states, most with political backgrounds. Some donkeys and some elephants. Some were very wealthy and some elderly and getting feeble, but all were nice people who were very interesting to talk to. When the Council came to town for meetings, it was a very big deal."

As for Mr. Biebel, Jewell didn't know him well, but her first impression of him was, "He always had ideas to contribute and he was very outspoken. Maybe he was a little bit cocky, slightly boastful, but the man always had a can-do attitude because, from what I could see, he always could do, and did."

Then Jewell got to know Fred and found him to be a man of action and consideration. He took her and several others to a meeting at the Republican National Committee (RNC) and introduced them to various powerful politicians. Jewell was floored. "He knew everybody, I mean absolutely everybody."

When the bicentennial celebrations were over, the Council remained. But there was no longer any need for PR personnel, so Jewell took a job with an attorney.

After the excitement of the previous year, she realized she was going to die a very slow, very agonizing death of sheer boredom. Then, one afternoon, at the end of August 1980, the phone rang. It was Fred Biebel.

"Jewell, Fred."

"Fred, hi! How's it going?"

"Good. Like your new job?"

"I hate it," she confided.

"Wanna work with me?"

"Yes, of course, are you kidding? I'd love to. What are you--"

"Electing a president. We're going to get Ronald Reagan elected. I'm coming to D.C. to set up an office at the RNC. We just took the New Hampshire Primary and we're going all the way."

"Oh my goodness. But Fred, what do I tell my boss? I just started here."

Fred called Jewell's boss to explain why he couldn't possibly pull off this most important election without her, and he was so charming that her new employer decided he was thrilled with the opportunity to contribute a valuable member to the team. With nothing but good wishes and exclamations for a great win, he let Jewell head out his door and right on over to Fred's the very next day. It was Monday, September 1, 1980. They had just eight weeks to get the job done.

Like so many others with whom Fred Bibel came in contact, Jewell's life changed from that moment on. An entirely new world opened up for her. Previously, she had held what she called "fairly low-level" jobs. No one can say with certainty that she would have continued typing endless, lifeless papers for the patent attorney, or whether she would have moved on and found something more suitable to support herself and her kids.

However, it is fair to say that she wouldn't have met her husband, who was deeply immersed in politics. And she probably would not have ended up at $1,000-a-plate dinners with people like Ed Meese, Counselor to the President. It is quite likely she would not have been entertained by the stand-up comic presentation of James Brady in her almost daily conversations with the White House Press Secretary. And you definitely could make money on a bet that she never would have witnessed the otherwise difficult Maureen Reagan, literally twirling and dancing into her meetings with Fred because Maureen thought Fred was the bees knees and she didn't care who knew it.

It's also safe to say Jewell would not have attended parties on the presidential yacht, The Sequoia, or been privy to the development of the innermost strategy sessions of the RNC.

When Jewell said yes to Fred, she took the same gamble that he did. There was no guarantee that they would win the election and that she would have a job after November 4th. But there wasn't any way she was going to miss out on the action or an opportunity to work with the human dynamo. Little did she know what she was getting herself into. Even though Jewell had seen him at the BTOC meetings and some of the festivities that resulted from their efforts, she hadn't yet worked directly *with* Fred.

The man she thought was simply a capable and confident guy turned out to be a veritable force of nature. And, according to her, one of the kindest people on the planet. But that was a world view of her entire interaction with him that extended over the eight years and multiple projects they worked on together.

Right now, they had a Herculean task in front of them, and the only way to pull it off was to work almost around the clock, seven days a week. Because, in addition to the campaign for Reagan, Fred was the representative of the RNC to the Inaugural Committee.

The preparation for a Presidential Inaugural begins up to a year-and-a-half before the actual event and is overseen by the Joint Task Force - Armed Forces Inaugural Committee, which is in charge of all military and ceremonial support. Regardless of who wins the election, there are literally hundreds of thousands of details that have to be in place. Yet nothing can be finalized until the election has taken place and the President-elect has created his own Presidential Inaugural Committee. Even a partial list of the kinds of things that need to be dealt with is daunting to contemplate:

Personnel:

• Job descriptions
• How many people
• Who should be hired
• How many members of the civilian corps will be used
• Who is paid, who is volunteer
• How to represent the Army, Air Force, Navy, Marine Corps & Coast Guard
• What sort of escorts are needed for VIPs
• Define the protocol for outgoing dignitaries, and President

Special Dinners: Security, Catering, Design, Construction, Traffic & Parking:

• President Elect and Family Reception
• Vice President and Family Reception
• First Ladies Dinner
• Co-Chairmen's Reception
• VIP and Distinguished Guests Dinner
• Special Candle Light Dinner

Press Box:

- Domestic TV, radio & pencil press
- International TV, radio & pencil press

Fire Works:

- What company, what kind, launched from where, paid for by whom

Activities:

- Allocation of tickets - Determined in conjunction with the Secret Service
- Security interface with FBI on all logistics and participants for the following:
- Fund raising projects, anticipated income, budgets
- Length of the Parade
- Length & number of bleachers
- Design & creation of Reviewing Stand
- The number of bands in the Parade /How to deal with those that are turned down
- The number of divisions in the Parade
- The order of appearance in the Parade
- The order of importance of the VIPs in the Parade
- The number of floats that will be allowed
- Creation of 10 to 13 Inaugural Balls - Design & Execution of each one
- Which locations can handle the largest crowds
- Souvenir design & creation for the ball patrons
- What guest actors or performers will be appearing
- Design & production of medals for the President & Vice President
- License plates and their distribution among VIPs with special provision that they can be used on the cars for only 30 days during and after the Inaugural

There were even stranger things to contemplate. The trees along the parade route had to be sprayed so that birds wouldn't alight in them and make a mess on the bleachers below. Flame throwers and the personnel trained to use them had to be available in case of ice and snow along the roadways. All of which meant that Fred had to have regular meetings with representatives of the military, a dizzying array of government officials and members of the Democratic National Committee. Plus attending to all the other activities he had to create and shepherd to completion.

Fred Biebel with assistant Jewell Duvall

The details of what needed to happen, the parallel development of so many disparate elements was so diabolically complex that Fred insisted that, as his Special Assistant, Jewell have her desk inside his office. That made her uncomfortable as she was then privy to all the meetings, plans and private conversations with a lot of very important people. However, Fred wanted someone he knew he could trust and who would be loyal to him. Jewell was the right choice.

Fred and Jewell were also involved with the Reagan State Chairmen, Regional Political Directors, Speakers Bureau, and everyone else involved with the campaign. At that time, Drew Lewis was the interim RNC Chairman, and they would frequently have working dinners with him and other staff members to work on strategy and scheduling.

Finally came the greatest of all days. They won the 1980 election in a landslide against President Carter. All of the hard work had paid off, but it was only a prelude to what was to come.

If they thought the run-up to the election had been maniacal, the race to the Inaugural was conducted at supersonic speeds. The day after the election, they started the move to the Inaugural Committee Headquarters at 2nd and T St. SW.

In the midst of that chaos, Jewell came down with pneumonia, but she battled back and hit the ground running after only a week. Fred was named one of three directors of the inaugural, but, as usual, he was charged with the burden of the prime responsibilities. As Executive Director, he was there to do the actual work. There were multiple assistants and helpers, but all the major logistics, details, decisions, and direction were on his shoulders.

Here again, the knowledge of how to shapeshift by knowing when to blend in and when to step to the forefront stood Fred in very good stead.

"I have always respected my bosses or people who held a superior political position," Fred explains. "Both of the other Directors, Bob Grey and Charlie Wick, were also appointed by the President.

"But they could pick up the phone and call Ronald Reagan; I couldn't do that. I respected that they were his friends and operated in a different league than I did. They were appointed to lend prestige and respect to the Inaugural. Charlie Wick knew the California players, Bob Grey knew the Washington D.C. players. Consequently, the two of them were a perfect match for the Inaugural."

There were approximately twelve thousand people involved in the preparation of the inaugural and the events raised over $90,000,000 for the Inaugural Committee.

To help out, Fred hired Kay Ford as Personnel Director to staff the committee. He had a military aide working with him as well. They only had six weeks to pull off the Inaugural. Twenty-four hours a day, seven days a week wasn't nearly enough time. Most of the time, the stress was merely unrelenting. On occasion, when things went wrong, it escalated into unbearable. As with any major publicly staged event, that was just par for the course.

Even the Master Shapeshifter couldn't be in forty-three places at once, however desperate the throngs were to see him. Every nuance of every decision made by everyone working on the Inaugural had to be vetted by Fred.

The level of activity was amazing. People didn't walk down hallways --they *ran* and they were multi-tasking as they went. No small accomplishment when you realize the hallways were lined every day, all day, with people waiting to have the Executive Director sign off on something. The ever-present line wrapped all the way around the floor and back to the cafeteria.

Fred had a system worked out with Jewell. While he was on the phone barking orders or coaxing committees into higher productivity, each person in the line could come in for no more than five minutes. It sounds insane--and of course it was--but it was also incredibly exciting and exhilarating.

Inaugural Parade Presidential Reviewing Stand

Fred, Jewell, and Kay may have looked like hell, but all three of them were in heaven. It was even better when Violet and the whole family came down. Though he couldn't really spend time with them, knowing they were there sharing in the greatest triumph of his career was a grounding force for him.

And then, because the Universe decided that he didn't have enough to do, Fred got a very special, high priority request. Well, not so much a request as a demand. One that could not be ignored and had to be accomplished in three days. The project was the creation of a suite of high-end offices in Washington. For the Committee Chairman responsible for one very special aspect of the Gala for President Reagan's Inaugural.

"I have known quite a number of chairmen over the years," Fred mused. "And, certainly, I've held the title myself on numerous levels, but this ultra-special, well-appointed office space was to be used by The Ultimate Chairman of the Board, Frank Sinatra."

Because of Reagan's previous career as an actor and his huge assortment of friends in the entertainment industry, a large number of Hollywood celebrities would be participating. Frank had actually asked to be in charge of the entertainment. Fred's instructions were to create the offices and get it done over the weekend.

Finding a site was no problem. In fact, there was a group of buildings located on 4th Street in Washington that had been used during the construction of the Pentagon. They looked like large Army barracks.

It was a Thursday afternoon and the clock was ticking. So Fred contacted one of the local Army brass and, along with one of his assistants, they toured four or five buildings to find the right spot for Sinatra's offices.

"I couldn't believe my eyes," said Fred. "Inside it was pitch black. The building, at least half an acre long, was loaded floor to ceiling with kitchen utensils that must have come out of every Army kitchen in the country and placed there for storage. As we walked down a narrow aisle, a cat jumped out and almost gave me a heart attack. It was the spookiest place I'd ever seen."

For the first time in his life, Fred realized that he didn't have to convince, cajole or coerce anyone into any thing. He now had the power of the President behind him, so he immediately instructed the Army officer to have the place cleaned out by that evening. When the officer asked where he should put the stuff, Fred told him that was his problem and his responsibility.

Within minutes, trucks, soldiers, and hordes of army staff descended on the place. Within hours, there was nothing left but the four walls and the ceiling.

Now came the tricky part. How to create a luxurious interior. In two days. Over a weekend. Scant weeks before the official Inaugural on which every single contractor in D.C. and Virginia was already working.

Fred's options were limited. He called the woman who was in charge of the General Services Administration, explained what he needed, and was most emphatic about the fact that he needed it at once. She agreed to meet him at the facility and, having looked around, said that she would get at it. But clearly, the urgency of Fred's need escaped her.

So Fred spelled it out for her in no uncertain terms. "This place has to be ready for occupation by Frank Sinatra on Monday morning at 9 o'clock.

"I need electricians, carpenters, tapers, painters, plumbers, rugs, furniture, potted plants and paintings from the art gallery on the walls. I need multiple crews of workers starting now and they will be working 24 hours around the clock until Monday morning. Get it?"

She didn't. And she said so. It couldn't be done and that was that. Fred blew his stack. "You're the damn chief of the GSA and you're telling me that you are saying no to the President of the United States?"

Fred finally succeeded in browbeating the woman into bringing in a crew, but they didn't even show up until mid-day on Friday. Knowing that the odds were against him, Fred checked back in later that afternoon. Next to nothing had been accomplished. Livid, Fred called the GSA Chief and told her that he would do the job himself.

Fred turned to the assistant for the name of the contractor he had put in charge of building the reviewing and press stands. Lady Luck was looking out for Mr. Biebel that day--as it turned out, the firm was one of the largest construction companies in Washington and eager to rise to the challenge.

Within thirty minutes, the construction company's president was in his office. Fred outlined what he needed and made sure it was understood that he now had forty-eight hours in which to get it done. Seventy-five men showed up almost immediately and set to work.

Then, Fred talked with a Navy supply officer and told him he needed enough government furniture to outfit a suite of ten offices and a reception area: carpets, desks, chairs, file cabinets, end tables and lamps.

Frank Sinatra and Peggy Venables

Next, Fred called the National Gallery of Art directly, once again invoking the power of the President. He explained that he needed to borrow some lovely paintings to hang on the walls. Finally, he had one of his assistants call the Botanical Gardens and ask to borrow trees and potted plants. Both requests were quickly filled.

They got the place ready five hours ahead of schedule. By 4 o'clock Monday morning everything was in place.

Wanting to do something special for Frank Sinatra, Fred contacted Peggy Venables, who was in charge of having the Inaugural vanity licenses plates made. He asked her to go to the local jail and have one made for Frank Sinatra. Several of Sinatra's people arrived to start work and, when Frank himself showed up, she presented it to him. Fred received a call from one of the secretaries saying that Sinatra wanted to meet him, but Fred had already lost valuable days on the side project and simply couldn't justify the time to go down and meet him.

As it turns out, that brief tour of his offices was the only time The Chairman of the Board was in the building. He had walked in and through and right back out again, never to return.

In the category of what goes around comes around, Fred found out in February that the woman from the GSA was being fired. Her last official, perhaps spiteful act, was to send him a bill for $50,000 for the alleged work her crew never actually did. In red ink, the word **URGENT** was stamped right across the top. Clearly, immediate action was required. So, as quickly as he could, Fred stuffed the bogus bill in a desk drawer and, for all anyone knows it sits there still.

Fortunately for Fred, his old-time friend, Jo McKenzie, had also come to Washington to help out at her own expense. For six months. Fred and Jo had known each other for over thirty years. They first met in the Bill room at the State Capitol when she was a clerk. Later, Jo's star also rose and Fred named her as his personal successor to the Republican Chairmanship where she become a National Committeewoman. Fred got a huge kick out of Jo, as did most of the people who met her. She was dynamic, flamboyant, and a very, very smart politician.

Way back when Fred was still President and CEO of PACE, Jo and her husband, Bob, came to him to seek his advice. They were going to be opening a restaurant and, with all Fred's contacts in the liquor industry, they were looking for someone who could help them choose which wines to buy to create a truly superior wine cellar.

Fred made a few calls and Jo's and Bob's endeavor succeeded beyond even their wildest dreams. Describing her management style Fred said, "Jo ran the place with military precision and a passion for perfection. She wanted the job done more than right, she wanted it done with distinction and elegance."

Their establishment became renowned as the four-star Copper Beech Inn in Ivoryton, Connecticut. Now under different management, the Copper Beech remains a four-star inn and restaurant.

For Jo McKenzie, Jewell Duvall, and Kay Ford, not to mention the thousands of others who were hard at work, the Inaugural was an over-the-top unqualified success.

Fred's kids and even two of his grandchildren remember being treated like royalty throughout all the festivities surrounding the Inaugural. Karen and her kids, Jimmy and Jennifer, got to sit directly across from the Presidential reviewing stand and gaze at Fred and Violet as they sat directly behind the man who was about to be sworn in as the 40th President of the United States.

Regardless of the political machinations that were alleged to have been in play in the background, Karen remembers the announcement made just twenty minutes after Reagan's Inaugural Address as one of the most emotional in her life. The American hostages held by Iran for 444 gruesome days had just been released.

In hindsight, Fred wished more than anything that he could talk to and thank his ancestors for the miraculous world he and his family were privileged to be a part of.

CHAPTER 15
Deputy Chairman

Bill Brock, a former U. S. Senator from Tennessee, was Chairman of the Republican National Committee from 1977 to 1981, which put him in that all-important position during Ronald Reagan's campaign for the Presidency.

Once Reagan defeated incumbent Jimmy Carter, many people wanted to be appointed to Cabinet positions and Brock was one of them. Following the inauguration in January 1981, Brock was named U.S. Trade Representative, and he served until 1985. In Reagan's second term, he was named Secretary of Labor from 1985 to 1987.

As proof that politics does indeed make strange bedfellows, while the campaign was being waged, Brock claimed he was going to be neutral. He really wasn't, and everybody--meaning all of Reagan's campaign staff--knew he would have preferred George Bush by a mile. Why then, after the election, would Brock be appointed by Reagan to serve in not one, but two cabinet positions? Party loyalty. The ability to let old slights and non-issues slide into the past. Blood is thicker than water and party blood can be positively viscous at times. Once the election was over, it was time for Reagan to surround himself with talented people and Bill Brock was one of them.

However, that didn't mean he had to give him special treatment beforehand, so as soon as Reagan won the primaries and knew he was going to win the election, he forced Brock out of Republican Headquarters. Then he plunked Drew Lewis, his campaign manager from Pennsylvania, and Fred Biebel into the Party's offices. Drew was acting Chairman of the Republican Party and Fred was his Deputy. From the middle of a funky gymnasium floor in New Hampshire to official Party Headquarters in Washington, D.C., Fred had done fairly well for himself in the last year or so.

There is a natural rhythm and cadence to the way the political process flows. The run-up to an election has its own kind of sprint-like quality, followed by a hard push to make it through the Inaugural. As the Inaugural winds down, the President-Elect's team begins to focus on setting the direction for the next phase of the journey, which has everything to do with who is going to be named National Chairman of the Republican Party. Bill Brock was going to have a Cabinet position, as would Drew Lewis, since Reagan was going to name him Transportation Secretary.

That left a number of individuals who were interested in the Chairmanship. Ultimately, the deliberations came down to three people. The first candidate was Dick Richards, a Mormon out of Salt Lake City who was a very close friend of Reagan's and had been his number one supporter in 1976, prior to his second attempt at the Presidency.

The second person was Frank Farhrenkopf, Chairman of the Nevada Republican Party and a very good friend of Fred Biebel's. The third person interested in the Chairmanship was, of all people, Fred Biebel himself.

Fred's buddy, Frank Fahrenkopf, claimed he was supporting Senator Paul Laxalt for the position. Laxalt knew and worked with Reagan when he was Governor of California. Laxalt had not only been the one to nominate Reagan in 1976 and 1980 (and would do so in 1984)

130

he also served as national chairman for three of Reagan's presidential campaigns. So, Reagan invented a new post called the General Chairman of the Republican Party, and named Laxalt to that position. Even though it officially ranked above the Party Chairmanship, the title was actually an honorific one.

Fred's name was bandied about fairly strongly for a while because he had built a reputation as someone who could and would move heaven and earth to get a job done. However, Fred knew that, among the innumerable variables to be considered when determining the right candidate for the Chairmanship, was the comfort level the President had with the person at the helm of the Party. Fred withdrew his name, realizing there was really only one candidate who fit the bill. Dick Richards had been friends with and an unqualified supporter of Reagan since 1976. That was the year that Fred had thrown his support and all thirty-five of Connecticut's delegates behind Gerald Ford.

Then something unusual happened. It was one of those things that escaped even the uncanny knowing that Fred seemed to possess about upcoming events. Bill Casey had been named as Director of the CIA--no big surprise there. The odd part was that once he had been named Chief Spook, he started to push for Fred to become Deputy Chairman of the National Republican Committee. Fred was floored that Casey wasn't going after someone he had worked more closely with or perhaps knew better. Then again, there were lots of things that Bill Casey did that nobody could explain. Certainly, Fred wasn't going to argue. He was appointed Deputy Chairman and directed to work closely with Dick Richards, something he looked forward to with great anticipation.

Jewell Duvall continued her job as Special Assistant to Fred when he became Deputy Chairman. Along with others who had worked for him over the years, she marveled at his ability to forget past wrongs and help people out. The man simply did not hold grudges.

Political cartoon published in the Bridgeport Post

"It was amazing to watch," Jewell said. "Everyone came to him for referrals and contacts. Without fail, he helped everyone who asked, including those people who didn't always deserve it. He always said 'If you can help someone, why not?'"

Therein lies some of the special magic of Fred Biebel. He was a grass roots organizer even when he was functioning on the national level. It was part of what made him so successful. Fred understood how to relate to individuals as people, and he understood that the definition of a good deal was when all parties walked away feeling as though they had both benefited from the deal.

While living in Washington, Fred had to maintain two homes, one in D.C. and his home with Violet and the kids in Connecticut. He flew back as often as he could and, many times, Violet would travel down to D.C. with their kids' children or grandchildren to visit and see the sights.

One might think that the pace of life would have slowed just a little bit after the maniacal intensity of the election and inaugural activities were over. With Fred functioning as liaison to the White House and Deputy National Chairman, just the opposite was true. It was left to him to fete anyone and everyone with whom the White House or the Party needed to interact. Also known as party patronage, it is how the process by which the wheels of government continue to move in a specific direction or, conversely, change direction as needed. So the same day Fred was nominated as Deputy Chairman, his social life moved over into the fast lane and stayed there.

The situation was reminiscent of the time that Fred had worked for Searle Pinney, when Searle was State Chairman. This time, it was Dick Richards who was working the legislative side of Capitol Hill. So it was up to Fred to utilize his persuasive powers on whatever issue was at hand. He wined and dined every dignitary, business contact, seeker of favors, committee member, Ambassador, congressman and senator in town. That included breakfast meetings, lunches, afternoon cocktail parties, dinners, receptions, galas, concerts, special events and theater performances. He even brought visiting European dignitaries to the circus when it was in town.

One of the pleasant respites from the exhausting round of entertaining and persuading that Fred looked forward to were his times with his old friend, Bill Middendorf, at the Metropolitan Club. The two men could meet for a quiet drink and their favorite pastime - talking politics. Both of them were absolutely dedicated to what they considered to be the bedrock values of the Republican Party: free market society, free enterprise, private property rights, an independent judiciary, constitutionalism and a strong defense.

As with many people who work at high power and high intensity jobs, most of Fred's friends were people he worked with during his sixteen hour, six days a week job. There weren't a lot of other options. It is a testament to Fred's character that the purely social friendships he had during those crazy years also lasted for many decades.

Fred Biebel with Ambassador William Middendorf

Friends like Park Shaw and his wife, Nancy. Even though they had moved to Arizona thirty years earlier, the two men remained close and, to this day, still talk at least once a week. What do they talk about? If you have to ask the question, you haven't been paying attention.

When the two couples used to travel together, Vi and Nancy would go off and entertain themselves. It wasn't as if both women weren't also politically active and aware--they just didn't feel the need to be placed on IV drips of the stuff while on vacation.

Park was and remains a huge admirer of Fred. Of the sixty years they've known each other, Park says they haven't had a single disagreement. For his part, Fred is proud of the fact that Colonel Park, U.S. Army, Ret., has been to 113 countries around the world, and brags that his best friend has also been a Rotarian for 50 years and never missed a meeting.

Not only that, Park found a way to make up for the fact that Fred got rejected all those years ago when he tried to enlist in the army. The last time Vi and Fred went to Arizona to visit, "the Colonel" as Fred refers to him with a salute, Park held a public ceremony. He made Frederick K. Biebel an honorary Colonel of the Arizona Guard, complete with applets and a sword that just happens to be longer than Fred is tall.

In both Fred's personal and professional relationships, mutual respect has always been a core value. Ms. Aretha Franklin sang about it, everybody talks about how rare it is these days, but that crucial quality is something that has been accorded to this unique political operative throughout his career as has been demonstrated by his life story. Chris DePino, the Republican Chairman of Connecticut in 2000, provided a perfect example of that respect in action.

While onlookers often see only an opportunity for the party faithful to party hearty, there are many politicos who see their respective National Conventions as their moment in the sun. If you're a stay-at-home mom or dad, an enterprising but unrecognized worker in a corporation, an employee who has offered nothing but top level service for not a lot of money, you will understand how powerful the simple offer of acknowledgement can be. How gratifying it can be to stand shoulder to shoulder with others who have shared the same experience and celebrate your world.

For the delegates, a national convention is a time when all the thankless work, late nights, stressed out strategy sessions, missed holidays, horrid food, hard fought battles and endless wrangling have paid off. A time when individual contributions and sacrifices have manifested into the reality of a candidate running for the highest elective office in the land.

It can also lead to major advancement in one's political career because of the exposure and networking that goes on behind the scenes.

To be willing to give that privilege away is an extraordinary gift. In July of 2000, The Connecticut Republican Chairman did just that. You would be hard pressed to find a Republican in office who wasn't aware of Fred's extraordinary attendance record for the National Convention. Twelve Republican Conventions in a row. Is there anyone else on either side of the aisle who can say the same?

At that time, Fred was not serving in any political capacity that would have entitled him to attend. The following year, his thirteenth convention, Fred did attend as an elected delegate. But that was in the future. This was convention number 12 and Chris DePino didn't want to see Fred's streak broken. Incredibly, he insisted Fred go in his place. "I gave up my spot because I wanted to honor him," said DePino. Now that's respect.

Sometimes, the quality of respect is demonstrated by coming through for the people who have believed in you. Meeting and exceeding their expectations for you. Jewell Duvall had worked for Fred for over eight years. When he decided to leave Washington to establish a consulting business with Ed Rollins, Jewell knew what she had to do. It was time to find a position that would provide her retirement money and security but she wanted to stay in government.

As in the way of all things relating to Fred Biebel, there was yet another odd coincidence. Jewell Duvall and Donna Miklus knew of one another through Fred, but had never met. When Fred left Connecticut for D.C., Donna went to work for the Department of Commerce in Hartford under the newly appointed Malcolm Baldridge. When things reversed and Fred left Washington to return to Connecticut, Jewell went to work for the Department of Commerce under Baldridge in D.C.

Jewell became a leader in her own right. She moved on to become the Director of Consumer Affairs and, following in Fred's organizational footsteps, was in charge of the 75th Anniversary Celebration of the Department of Commerce. It was a week-long event that involved 250,000 employees worldwide. When Malcolm Baldridge was succeeded by William Verity, Jewell was Promoted to Chief of Protocol. Nobody was more proud of what she had achieved than Fred.

CHAPTER 16
The CIA

Most of the time, a stereotype is just that. Some projected image or conception of specific traits based on inadequate knowledge or even inappropriate innuendo. Then again, sometimes it appears to be right on the money.

Consider William Casey. Bill to those who knew him. An odd and often mysterious man. Yes, he had worked for the agency that was the predecessor of the CIA. In fact, he'd worked for the OSS (Office of Strategic Services) for most of World War II. He'd sussed out who and what Fred Biebel was about in a heartbeat and brought him to Reagan's side. Then, Casey had served as Director of the CIA for four years.

Clearly, that pedigree required a man who displayed great acuity, discernment, and penetrating insight. So how do you explain Casey's stereotypical presentation of the absent-minded, mumble-mouthed spy? His apparent lapses of awareness, the times he seemed oblivious to who and what was around him, were antithetical to the man's reputation.

The mumbled, hard-to-understand words were easy enough to explain--it was simply his style of speech. After spending time with him, his mouthful-of-marbles words became more discernible. It was a little like listening to a foreign accent, eventually the awkward cadences disappeared and his meaning became clear. However, there were times when the man just appeared to be, for lack of a better term, out of it.

A case in point. In 1980, before the election had taken place, Fred Biebel and Bill Casey took a trip together to St. Charles, Illinois.

They were attending a meeting of State Republican Chairmen at a resort called Pheasant Run, located not far from Chicago's O'Hare Airport. Fred brought Vi along and they were joined by Drew Lewis (who became CEO of the Union Pacific Railroad after his stint as Secretary of Transportation). At that time, Lewis was attending the meeting as head of Reagan's campaign organization in Pennsylvania.

At the week-long conference, the business and strategy meetings among the Republican State Chairmen were broken up by organized lunches and dinners. Every day for the entire week, Drew Lewis, Bill Casey, and Fred and Violet Biebel sat at the same table and carried on lively conversations about politics, places, and the people they knew.

When the conference ended, the foursome piled into a cab, with Casey in the front seat and set out for the airport. As they climbed out of the car, Bill turned to Drew, indicating Violet with his chin and said, "Who is that woman?"

Lewis looked at Casey to see if he was serious, then responded, "That's Violet, Fred's wife. You've been sitting next to her for a week." Bill looked a little bemused, shook his head, and turned to enter the terminal.

Arriving at the airline counter, Casey reached into his pocket for his ticket and came up empty. He checked his coat while everybody helped search his bags and his briefcase. But the ticket was nowhere to be found.

Fred called the resort and asked the manager to send someone to look in Casey's room for the missing ticket. While he waited, Fred mused about the apparent contradictions of his colleague. The manager reported that they had searched everywhere and found nothing.

The only thing to do was buy another ticket. The snag in that idea was that Casey not only didn't have his ticket, he didn't have any money with him. Drew Lewis paid for the ticket and, in the ensuing reassembling of everybody's luggage and coats, Casey promptly misplaced it again. This time, it was recovered in short order and Violet literally pinned it to his coat so he wouldn't lose it.

Bill Casey created and ran a dynamically powerful and intelligent campaign that brought Ronald Reagan to the White House. He'd been Chairman of the Securities and Exchange Commission. He was director of the biggest intelligence operation on the planet. The man was known to be brilliant. He was also a millionaire. But he would take off for a meeting in Europe without a penny in his pocket.

There also seemed to be something amiss with Bill Casey and airports. One time, he took a taxi to an airport and, upon arrival, discovered that he didn't have enough money to pay the fare. He explained that he was the Director of the CIA and then asked the cabbie to send him a bill, promising to mail him a check. Apparently, he was convincing, because the driver let him go. Was the bill ever sent? If so, was it paid? The answer is probably classified.

Many months after the Illinois conference, Violet told Fred that he had received a call from the FBI office in Atlanta. It seems an agent there was most anxious to talk with him about something extremely important.

Vi was anxious, but Fred was unruffled. Somebody, somewhere, needed a favor or wanted his help with something. He returned the call and got the agent on the phone. The man's attitude was abrupt and not a little sharp. He wanted to know Fred's exact whereabouts during the week of August 7, 1980.

The answer was simple and Fred responded immediately. He told the agent he had been at a meeting at Pheasant Run in Illinois.

When asked just how he was able to answer so quickly and specifically, Fred replied that the date was stuck in his mind.

Instantly suspicious, the FBI agent pressed him for an explanation. Fred felt his heart step up a beat or two. That's silly, he told himself, he hadn't done anything wrong.

Fred explained that he had been at a meeting of all of the Republican State Chairmen in the country. The agent demanded to know who had gone with him. With one part of his brain, Fred answered the man's questions; the rest of his mind was searching desperately for any possible reason for the intense scrutiny.

"I was with Drew Lewis, who is now Secretary of Transportation," he said testily, "Bill Casey, CIA Director, my wife, and about forty other chairmen from across the country."

Not good enough. The agent continued to grill Fred, seeking details about when he went home, who he went with, and where else they might have gone. The agent insisted there must be a more plausible explanation for Fred's ability to recall such detail about an arbitrary week that was many months in the past.

Likely due to the fact that he was under duress, Fred didn't stop to think about who Bill Casey was and what he did, on or off the record. The agent kept pushing. Finally Fred got what he terms "hot under the collar" and told the agent that he remembered every damn detail of the occasion because Bill Casey had lost his damn airline ticket and after obtaining a second one, lost that one, too.

Maybe it was Fred's refusal to be intimidated, but he finally convinced the agent he was absolutely certain of his story.

The agent told Fred he would have to go the FBI offices in Atlanta, Georgia, to give a deposition. Fred had reached his limit. "If you want to take a deposition, you can take one here in Connecticut. You have FBI agents all over the country." With that, he hung up the phone. Hard.

The following day, the same agent called back, saying a decision had been made to accept a statement from Fred over the phone. Some time later, Fred thought he figured out what the FBI had been after.

The ensuing months following the ticket debacle encompassed the return of the hostages from Iran. It appeared that the FBI thought Casey had gone to Paris on a secret mission, even before the election, and had used the Pheasant Run conference as a cover.

Well, if that's what they thought, then they were dead wrong, because even if Casey couldn't identify his lunch partners that week, Fred Biebel was one hundred percent clear on who he'd been sitting next to.

CHAPTER 17
The Hell With The Super Bowl,
My Chauffeur Is Trying To Kill Me

In January 1982, Fred decided to take a long weekend in Connecticut. Things had been busy as all get out and he needed some peace and quiet. Toward that end, he decided he didn't want to deal with noisy and busy airports. Instead, he would take the opportunity to get some paper work done while he had the chauffeur--who had been assigned to drive him around Washington--drive him to Stratford instead.

Though his chauffeur was pleasant enough, the relationship wasn't the same as the one he'd had with Cliff. In fact, he had quit driving for Fred before Fred's life had escalated into the stratosphere. Cliff just needed some kind of structure and schedule he could count on. Truth be told, he had tried to quit a number of times. Unsuccessfully.

Summoning his courage, Cliff had told Fred that, after five years of driving everywhere at all hours, he thought he really needed a job that was little more nine to five. Fred nodded understandingly, then proceeded to "Biebelize" him.

"I understand what you're saying, but why don't you stay for just one more election campaign?" And then, "Just hang in there until we get this legislation through the Senate." And then, "Let's finish canvassing this portion of the state and I'll find someone to take your place."

Finally, the only way Cliff could get away was to go through Violet. He told her he was quitting and that he just didn't have the heart to tell Fred. He didn't mention the fact that he was afraid Fred would talk him out of it again. He figured she already knew that. It was thirty years before Fred and Cliff had a chance to see one another again. Both men had continued their careers and were retired. They had a great reunion and a lot of fun reminiscing about the good old days when gas prices were fifty-three cents and Cliff had a ringside seat for the endless verbal fisticuffs between Fred, John Bailey and Ella Grasso.

Fred's life had completely transformed since he and Cliff had crisscrossed Connecticut on a daily basis. For one thing, gas prices were more than double and, instead of being State Chairman working for the folks in Connecticut, he was Deputy National Chairman working for the folks in the White House.

The chauffeur who had been assigned to Fred by the Republican National Committee claimed to be a minister. Whether he was an ordained minister or a self-proclaimed one, Fred never knew. But he carried a bible with him everywhere he went. He had been driving Fred around D.C. for almost a year and had always been very reliable and polite.

It was early evening by the time they reached Connecticut. As Fred walked in his door that night, he could hear the phone ringing. Before he even had a chance to greet his wife, she pushed the phone at him with a surprised look on her face. "Fred, it's the Vice President." Fred's eyebrows disappeared into his hairline.

"Good evening Mr. Vice President, what can I do for you?"

As it turns out, it was more about what Vice President Bush could do for Fred. He was calling to ask if the Deputy Chairman wanted to accompany him to Super Bowl XVI at the Silverdome in Pontiac, Michigan. Fred would be his guest aboard Air Force II on Sunday morning out of Andrews Air Force Base.

Fred was thrilled by the invitation and accepted immediately. As he was unpacking and repacking his bags, Violet called upstairs to tell him the weather report had just announced that a big snowstorm was headed their way.

Fred Biebel with Vice President George H. W. Bush

Knowing that snow was an airline passenger's worst enemy, Fred decided to have his chauffeur--who was staying at a nearby motel--drive him back to Washington the next day. That way, he would be in town and ready to go to Andrews Air Force Base Sunday morning.

Connecticut weather is notorious for embodying a famous line that has been attributed to Mark Twain: "If you don't like the weather in New England, wait fifteen minutes." What Twain actually said in his incredibly funny lecture in New York City during the winter of 1876 runs more than a thousand words, but the witticism is fairly apt. Fred's drive home had been under clear skies, shortly after he received the Vice President's call, it started to storm.

At first, he thought he couldn't possibly make it back to Washington if the snow continued at the rate it was falling. Then the storm abated and he grew hopeful. But, during the night, the snow and wind grew progressively worse.

By Saturday morning, air travel was out of the question and Fred knew it would be tough going on the roads. Vi couldn't believe he was even going to try, but this was the invitation of a lifetime.

The San Francisco 49ers vs. the Cincinnati Bengals. At The Super Bowl. With the Vice President of the United States. Arriving on Air Force II. An entire battalion of southern rebels backed up by an armada of English frigates could try, but nothing was going to stop Frederick K. Biebel from making a run for it.

The chauffeur, with Fred in the back seat, got on the Interstate and, staying in the far right lane, slowly churned their way south. By the time they had gone a little over twenty miles, things had gotten very dicey. Just before the exit for Darien, Connecticut, a Valley Transit Company bus crashed into a car which then smashed into Fred's vehicle.

The chauffeur was unhurt, but Fred was injured. Someone called an ambulance and Fred was taken to Stamford Hospital, where they discovered he had two fractured ribs.

Before the ambulance arrived, Fred called his son Kevin, who managed to get to the scene of the accident in his four-wheel drive truck. The car was badly smashed and had to be towed, so Kevin picked up the driver and headed to the hospital to bring his father back to Stratford.

They delivered Fred to Violet's care at home, then Kevin took the chauffeur to the motel where he had stayed the previous night.

His instructions were to stay overnight, then take the train back to Washington and report to the RNC office on Monday morning.

Adding insult to injury, Fred had to call Vice President Bush with his regrets. He would not be joining him for Super Bowl XVI after all.

Fred couldn't bear to watch the game on television though he did see the final score. The 49ers had beaten the Bengals, 26 to 21. It had been a great game. A few weeks later, Bush presented him with an official Super Bowl Program, which he had autographed.

Fred took three days at home to recover from the accident, but he and Jewell were in constant touch. The chauffeur was on the payroll of the Republican National Committee and, though assigned as Fred's full-time driver, he did other chores and errands around the RNC office when Fred was out of town. Fred asked Jewell to keep an eye out for him on Monday and to give him some work to do until Fred returned to his office. When Fred got back to Washington, Jewell told him that the chauffeur had never reported back to work.

"Well," Fred responded, "I know he left Connecticut because I paid his hotel bill. And I know he ate pretty well while he was there, because I paid that bill, too."

They tried contacting him by phone, but got no response. Fred was ready to write him off, but Jewell realized she had to go through official channels. When she talked to the RNC's legal counsel, she was told to terminate him because he apparently had abandoned the job.

Ten days later, the chauffeur strolled casually into the office and asked for his paycheck. Jewell explained that he had been terminated. He hadn't returned as instructed, he hadn't even called to check in. They had no choice but to assume he had quit.

He exclaimed, "Oh, Jewell, I got hurt real bad. I've seen my doctor. I've been in bad shape."

Jewell responded, "Well, you don't look too bad right now. What happened?"

The chauffeur kept repeating that he'd been badly hurt, though he couldn't seem to explain his injuries or remember the name of the doctor who treated him. All he wanted, he said, was his paycheck. Jewell paid him for the time that he was owed. He took the check and angrily left the office.

Meanwhile, Fred had been commuting on weekends between Washington and Connecticut via Sikorsky Memorial Airport. Almost a month after the scene in the office with the chauffer, Fred received a call just as he entered his house on Friday evening. His administrative aide in D.C. had some shocking news to deliver.

The aide explained that the office had received a call from the noted columnist, Jack Anderson, who, at the time, was writing for Parade Magazine. Anderson said that he had gotten a call from Biebel's ex-driver, who claimed he was going to kill Fred. He had also made some vague threats against President Reagan. A call had already been placed by the GOP to the security officers in Washington.

They wanted Fred to stay put and not to leave the house under any circumstances. Within thirty minutes, the Connecticut State Police and the Stratford Police converged on Fred's home.

"It was a scene straight out of Hollywood," Fred remembers. "As the State Police questioned me about my ex-driver, they mentioned that he had told Anderson that he knew one of my aides was in love with him.

"After a good laugh, we decided that there was only one possible explanation," Fred said. "Jelly beans. During one of the political or social events my wife and I had attended in Washington, President Reagan had given me jars of jelly beans. He was famous for having those candies on his desk.

"Apparently, some people gave their jars away, which I guess the driver interpreted as a sign of someone being enamored of him."

The Stratford Police had determined that the driver lived in Washington, so they set up an operation in conjunction with Connecticut State Police to monitor all phone calls in case the chauffeur tried to get in touch with Fred by calling his Connecticut home. They coached Violet on what she should say to him and how to keep him talking while, on a separate phone, they could listen to the conversation.

150

Fred's fear was that the "minister" knew where Fred and Violet lived because he had dropped Fred at home before going to the motel. The authorities were just as concerned. There was an armed guard in the house in Stratford at all times, and the State Police escorted Violet and Fred everywhere they went, including when they walked the dog.

In the meantime, RNC security in Washington had been to Fred's apartment and installed all kinds of security measures to safeguard him when he returned.

Within a day or two, while Fred was still recuperating at home, the phone call came. Fred said, "As best as I can recall, the conversation went like this:

"Hello, Mrs. Biebel, this is Fred's driver. I need $300.

"Violet asked, "Why do you need $300?"

He said, "I have to go to Chicago to see my daughter. She's been raped, so I have to go be with her."

Violet answered, "I'd be happy to help you. How can I get the $300 to you? Where are you?"

He replied, "I'm calling from a pay phone at the boat basin at Washington National Airport."

Violet repeated her question, "How can I get the money to you?"

Obviously, he hadn't thought the plan all the way through, so he told her that he would figure that out and call her back.

That was all the Stratford Police needed to hear. They called the Washington P.D. and, within fifteen minutes, the man was picked up at the boat basin.

"Sure enough" said Fred, "There he was in his car with a gun."

He was taken to jail and appeared in court the next morning. For reasons Fred never understood, he was not officially charged with anything and the judge simply let him go.

Fred and the authorities were all very concerned that the driver had been released. Nobody knew where he was. So, for a time, they kept the security measures in place in Connecticut and Washington.

Any time Fred had to go to the Legislative Office Buildings--either the Cannon Building or one of the Congressional buildings--an armed security guard accompanied him at all times.

Eventually, things calmed down since the man had disappeared. He was no longer living at his address in Washington and Fred fervently hoped that would be the last he would hear of him.

A long while later, Fred was in the process of designing a new medal for President Reagan. He had arranged to stay in Washington for the weekend to meet a representative of the Danbury, Connecticut, Mint to review some preliminary sketches. Violet had joined him there and Fred had arranged to have a business dinner for the three of them. Just before they left for the meeting, the phone rang. It was Fred's daughter, Kyle, calling from Connecticut. She was in tears.

Kyle was very frightened because calls had been coming in from all over the country from friends and colleagues of Fred's. They wanted to warn him that the networks were running a news story about Fred's ex-driver. The man was bragging to reporters that he was going to be on a TV program with prominent attorney F. Lee Bailey in which people were subjected to lie detector tests.

It seems Fred's former employee was offended by the accusations that he had threatened to kill Fred Biebel and the President. The story was sensationalized and Attorney Bailey was leveraging the publicity all day to build the hype for that night's program.

Fred was horrified. "So there we were, Violet and I, ready to go to dinner for a business meeting, and I was a nervous wreck. We got to the hotel, met the representative from the Mint and had a drink. I wasn't focused because my mind was on the upcoming TV program.

"I didn't want to cancel the meeting or the dinner, but the fact that this man had succeeded in making the threats a national story had me so on edge I couldn't function."

Fred realized he needed to explain what was going on. The gentleman from the Mint immediately offered to take them up to his room so they could watch the show.

"There we were, the three of us, sitting on this guy's hotel bed. We no sooner turned on the set than my ex-driver, big as life, appeared on screen."

The three of them watched, fascinated, as he got wired up for the polygraph and then Bailey started asking him all kinds of questions. Nobody remembers the specifics, but what Bailey was doing was establishing for the audience how a polygraph worked. He wanted them to see what the readout looked like when the driver was telling the truth and when he was lying. To accomplish that, the driver was asked his name and simple questions, such as what color shirt he was wearing. Then, he was forced to lie when he was instructed to say yes to a question such as, are you six foot nine inches tall.

Of course, the intent was to build suspense, so Bailey kept the ball rolling until finally, at very last moment, he got to the core issue and asked in a series of questions whether he had made the threats. Each time he answered, "No," the audience watched the needle spike like crazy. The "terribly wrongly accused" minister had just completely, dramatically, and unequivocally flunked the polygraph test in front of the entire country.

CHAPTER 18
Democracy To The World

Having been White House Liaison since 1983, Fred's new job was one he helped to create. In 1985, he co-founded a 501(c)(3)organization called the International Republican Cooperation Fund (IRCF). Fred was named Executive Vice President and Secretary Treasurer of the privately-funded group.

Steve Grant, the Capitol Bureau Chief for the Hartford Courant, said, "Frederick K. Biebel, the former Connecticut Republican Chairman, is working out of a suite of rooms, waging a little-noticed but well-financed campaign to promote conservative parties and democracy worldwide."

According to Fred, the inspiration for the organization came from a speech Reagan gave in 1982 to the British Parliament, when he called for a "crusade for freedom which would engage the faith and fortitude of the next generation."

One of Reagan's stipulations was that no government funds be used. This was the Republican Party reaching out to the world in an effort to share their conservative ideals. As such, no public monies would ever be expended in its operation.

Fred explained the IRCF this way, "We are trying to promote and advance democracy among all of the countries of the world on a people-to-people and party-to-party basis rather than a government-to-government basis.

"We are not in the business of trying to overthrow governments or telling other people how they should live, but we want to work together with like-minded political parties to promote our principles of democracy and free enterprise."

It may sound flip, but Fred's ability to throw amazing parties and events was a unifying force for the multinational groups of people he sought to engage. He knew that whenever people let their hair down, they tended to be more open and willing to entertain new ideas.

Fred used the occasion of the Republican Convention in Dallas to host the conservative leaders of two hundred countries from around the world. He created seminars that featured presentations by top officials like Ed Meese (the president's counselor) Secretary of State George Schulz, and Frank Fahrenkopf who was president of the Fund.

He also leveraged the affair by putting together a special edition of selected historical writings as a gift for each of the attendees. Over forty-two countries were represented, many of whom were new to the inner workings of the process of democracy. They got to witness the nominating ceremony and were also invited to briefings on American policy during the day.

"The history of these organizations," Fred explained, "proves that like-minded political parties can effectively organize for joint action. Political party leaders, unencumbered by the limits of governmental responsibilities, are far better able to forge alliances and bridge differences among the nations than are government officials."

Often, Fred would have up to ten foreign visitors a week stopping by his office. "I've had people come in from some of these struggling Third World countries and say, 'Tell me about this business of free enterprise and how you get it going' or 'Tell me, how do you raise funds for political campaigns, how do you go about registering voters?'"

Fred Biebel with Richard Allen and Frank Fahrenkopf

Political cartoon appearing in the Bridgeport Post

With his work at the IRCF, Fred was in his element. He had an opportunity to share his knowledge of how to set up telephone campaigns, how to stage debates that attracted the attention of the public and what constituted the basic elements of a local versus national campaign. He also got to talk politics with people like Margaret Thatcher, Jacques Toubon, a member of the French National Assembly, and John Gunner, then chairman of the British Conservative party.

"The leaders of the majority party in Great Britain or Australia or any of the other countries with parliamentary systems meet regularly with their prime ministers to formulate their government policy," said Fred, explaining how different systems function. "In the United States, the elected administration will attempt to carry out party programs, but the party leaders usually don't formulate policy on a day-to-day basis with the administration. Congress and the administration make the policy."

Brittish Prime Minister Margaret Thatcher with Fred and Violet Biebel

Fred traveled to Costa Rica and other countries to help promote free market economies and advise fledgling democracies. Later, the IRCF would be renamed the International Republican Institute. Though the name changed, the mission statement remained the same.

When Fred was Executive Director, the main focus of the group was Latin America. Once the Cold War was officially over, the organization sought to expand its scope world wide. The IRI is currently active in seventy-two countries.

As of this writing, not so coincidentally, Fred's old friend, Bill Middendorf, is the Secretary-Treasurer of the IRI and his buddy, Frank Fahrenkopf, remains on the Board of Directors. John McCain serves as Chairman the Board of Directors.

CHAPTER 19
Chief Justice For All - The Liberty Tour

For all of the years and all of the people he helped along the way, Fred Biebel was around sixty years old when he finally got his first mentor.

In 1985, Fred had the incredible honor of being appointed by Ronald Reagan as a Commissioner of the Bicentennial of the United States Constitution, headed by Chief Justice Warren Burger.

According to the Center for Civic Education, "At the first meeting of the Commission on the Bicentennial of the United States Constitution in July 1985, Chief Justice Warren E. Burger, Chairman, stated that the occasion should afford an opportunity for 'a history and civics lesson for all of us.'

The Commission intended to invite the country to participate in three years of celebration from 1987 through 1989. The goal was to create "plans and activities to commemorate the Bicentennial of the Constitution in 1987, emphasizing educational opportunities and the enlargement of public understanding and appreciation of the Constitution."

Fred was astonished that he was included on the committee. Of course, he had remained a Commissioner for the Bicentennial of the Original Thirteen States and was still working with them on events, but this was a whole other kettle of fish.

Political cartoon appearing in the Bridgeport Post

"I went on that Board with a lot of powerful people," Fred divulged. "At one point, I said to myself, man, I hope I can keep up with these guys. There were people like Teddy Kennedy, Phyllis Schlafly, Strom Thurmond, Lynne Cheney, the Attorney General of the United States, law professors, judges, I mean lots of very important people. And I was a nobody. But I soon learned that I could keep up with every one of them, and do a bang-up job, to boot."

There were hundreds of programs and projects created and a lot of money was spent on the celebrations. According to a New York Times article by Martin Tolchin in 1987, "The commission has spent $15 million of $25 million appropriated. 'The chief has been very frugal,' said one commission member, Lynne Cheney, who is chairman of the National Endowment for the Humanities. An additional $15 million is pending in the current appropriation bill."

The article went on to say that, to date, they had "spent $3 million on salaries; $2.7 million on instructional material and contests for high school students; $2 million on advertising; $600,000 on projects relating to a huge celebration in Philadelphia Sept. 17; $500,000 on pocket Constitutions; $400,000 on calendars; $200,000 for a 'teach-in,' and lesser amounts on a re-enactment of the Constitutional Convention, souvenirs, tree plantings and reprints. Among other activities, commission members themselves posed with Mickey Mouse at Disney World." More about the Mouse later.

Historians groused about the lack of scholarly representation, but Burger was more focused on bringing the power of the Constitution to the people through public awareness.

There were also complaints about how iron-fisted the Chief Justice was in his management of the Commission itself and the fact that he insisted the meetings be held "in secret". The "Chief", as he was known to everyone, defended the need for closed door sessions by claiming it was the only way to get the massive job done.

Warren E. Burger was an imposing figure and Fred found himself intimidated by the man, his office and the power he wielded. Fred was well aware that the Chief Justice had administered the Presidential Oath to Nixon in 1973, Ford in 1974, Carter in 1977, and Reagan in 1981 and 1985.

Additionally, Burger was well known for two traits in particular. He was incredibly strict and he disliked and distrusted the press to the point where he never, ever, gave a news conference. Not once.

"I was a bit fearful of him because he was so high and powerful," Fred admits. "Here was a man who didn't have to touch a doorknob, somebody would always open a door for him. He was a Justice for life, had his own dining room in the Supreme Court, his own Police Department, his own Fire Department, I mean he had a better job than the President of the United States.

"For some reason, he took a personal liking to me and appointed me to his Executive Committee and his Finance Committee. We just just naturally became close friends."

It's likely that Burger got a bead on Fred's work ethic and the fact that anything delegated to him was guaranteed to be done on time and often under budget

Fred and the Chief spent a lot of time together. They would have lunch and dinner in the Chief's private dining room, which was furnished with elegant antiques he had purchased from his own pocket.

"I would go over to spend time with him at the Supreme Court," Fred remembers with a smile. "As a matter of fact, I was able to drive my car right in the building, into the parking garage and there was a space set aside for me whenever I wanted to see him."

Though he appeared stern and tough, Violet really appreciated Burger's sense of humor. "Fred and I were having lunch with him in his private dining room, and I thought he was very funny," she said. Fred agreed, adding that the Chief could be particularly adept at delivering criticism by injecting the comment with humor.

"He had a very sharp wit and could be highly satirical. That said," Fred continues, "though he wasn't easily approachable, once you got to know him, he became very friendly and affable."

When asked what he learned from the Chief Justice, Fred surprisingly responds, "Love of country." Fred Biebel was a man who had devoted his time and talents to his country for all of his adult life. What could Burger possibly teach him about loving his country?

In a word, the "Constitution". Warren Burger believed in interpreting the Constitution as a strict-constructionist. Which, in essence means, that inferring ideas or interpretations outside of the exact wording of the document was tantamount to heresy. Fred was moved by how important it was to the Chief, that the privileges and freedom provided by the backbone of the country be taught to every young American.

It was Burger's position that the educational system of the United States had virtually betrayed the youth of the country by not teaching them about the core values and power bestowed by the Constitution.

The second thing Fred learned was not to trust the press. Though he never used the word hate, the enmity with which Burger regarded them was legendary.

The civility, camaraderie and cooperation Fred had experienced with colleagues and the press in his early years in politics had disappeared. He thinks, as many others do, it was when the corporations came in and the news became a money-making machine rather than a neutral franchise of people objectively reporting on people and events.

Fred couldn't change the tabloid quality of what passed for journalism, but he did end up providing the Chief Justice with what Burger himself considered to be one of the high points of the entire Bicentennial Celebration. As with so much of Fred's life, the entire chain of events was triggered by a mere coincidence.

"One day, I was at a meeting of the 13 States Commission which had nothing to do with the Federal Commission," he explains, "when one of the trustees mentioned that a guy by the name of Paul St. John, I think his name was, was bringing the Magna Carta from the Lincoln Cathedral in England to Oregon.

"And that's when I had a brainstorm. Maybe we should do something with the Magna Carta. It was the precursor of our Constitution.

"I went to run it by the Chief and I hit a nerve. I didn't realize that his love and study of the Constitution began when he was a youngster and had been given an assignment in school that had to do with the Magna Carta. He was enthralled by the idea that we could possibly display this valuable document."

There was a problem. Dealing with an antiquity of that caliber was going to cost money. A lot of it. And, as Fred puts it, "The Chief was very tight with the dough. We were spending federal funds and he was sensitive to any possible criticism."

Then Fred had the best-timed brainstorm of his entire career. "What if, what if, we could put together a world-class, once-in-a-lifetime exhibit that had all of our famous documents like the Constitution and the Bill of Rights--"

The Chief Justice was ecstatic. "Yes, absolutely, that would be worth the financial investment," and he began scribbling the names of documents on a pad of paper.

Ostensibly, there are only a handful of copies left in the world of the original Magna Carta. The first version of the document was more or less forced on King John in 1215 by the wealthy and powerful barons who were unhappy with his total and often despotic rule. The document sought to limit the King's powers and grant some authority to the feudal society. Throughout the years, there were a number of amended versions, but it is the one crafted in 1297 that, to this day, remains in the statute books of both England and Wales.

The copy that Fred was after was one of the originals from 1215. King John had given each baron a copy of the Magna Carta and only four or five of those remain in existence. Two of those copies, one of which had been damaged by a fire reside in England. The other was in perfect shape and that was the one Fred got his hands on.

From his work with BTOC, Fred had access to wonderful historians who could help them with the preparation of lectures and materials to accompany the exhibit. But the biggest boon to the project was the fact that the Chief Justice was also Chairmen Emeritus of the Smithsonian Institution. No other organization could manage the packing, moving, and presentation of such an awesome collection of American treasure.

The planning began in October, with the official opening held in March. The exhibit itself was carried through to September, which brought the time frame for planning and the execution of the Magna Carta project close to a year.

Though Fred's main job was still running the IRCF, the Bicentennial Commission had monthly as well as committee meetings, and the Chief had asked him to Chair the Magna Carta project. One stipulation Burger made was that the presentation had to be free and open to the public.

The next question was where to stage the presentation. They considered the Supreme Court Building, but the Chief Justice wanted to get it somewhere where more young people would have the opportunity to view it. Burger was absolutely determined to find a way to expose young and old to the historic documents.

Biebel Brainstorm Number Three. "What about a traveling exhibit?" Fred asked. The silence was deafening. How in the world could they do that? The sheer magnitude of the idea was overwhelming.

But the more he thought about it, the more he thought it could be done. The Chief wanted to know what that might cost. Fred estimated they would need something along the lines of five million dollars to cover everything from security, to high-tech, humidity controlled, bomb proof display cases.

The Chief said that, at that price, Fred would have to find a way to raise the money separately. Fred blinked, then said, okay, he'd handle it. Nobody could fundraise like Fred Biebel. His first thought was to talk to his old friend, Drew Lewis. Drew was back working in the private sector, so Fred called him and asked which corporate boards he was serving on. Drew told him he was on the Board of Directors for Ford and for American Express.

"Stop right there," Fred said. "Those are the guys I want."

Next, Fred put a team of people together to coordinate and execute all the details of the massive project and set up offices in the basement of his home in Stratford. Then he called in all of his contacts from the Bicentennial of the Original 13 States Commission and told them they were being given the opportunity of a lifetime. Literally a dream project for any historian.

Chief Justice Warren E. Burger with Fred Biebel

"We are going to put together a traveling display of artifacts and documents that define the very history of this country. Starting with the Magna Carta.

"The Smithsonian is on board and they will supervise all handling and design of the displays, but what say we make their job interesting, and come up with a knock-out list of materials?"

Which is just what they did. The list of items in what became officially known as "The Roads to Liberty Tour" included the following:

DOCUMENTS

Magna Carta - 1215

The Constitution of the United States of America
Pierce Butler (1744-1822) 1787. The next-to-last draft of the Constitution with changes inserted in Butler's handwriting.

The Declaration of Independence - 1776
A Dunlap Broadside is one of the first 200 copies of the Declaration of Independence, printed by John Dunlap of Philadelphia, the night of July 4, 1776.

The Articles of Confederation, 1781
The first constitution of the United States.

The Bill of Rights - 1791

The First Ten Amendments

Mayflower Compact - 1620
English common law transferred to America from an account by William Bradford - 1590-1657, Governor of Plymouth Colony.

The Fundamental Orders of Connecticut - 1638-1639
The first written constitution.

Magnalia Christi Americana - 1702
Cotton Mather (1663-1728), a leading Puritan clergyman of Boston wrote this history of New England.

History and Genealogy
By Rev. Thomas Hooker(1865)

Maps of Windsor, Wethersfield, and Hartford, Connecticut
Mid-1600s.

New York Weekly Journal - Nov. 11, 1734
*John Peter Zenger's anti-administration newspaper published this
editorial on freedom of the press just one week before his arrest for libel
by the colonial governor. His eventual acquittal was a major victory
for freedom of the press in the colonies.*

Pennsylvania Gazette - Feb. 9, 1747
Printed by Benjamin Franklin.

Original page from an English Bible - circa 1220
Copied by hand around the same time the Magna Carta was written.

The Resolution of May 15, 1770
Colonies assume the powers of government.

Boston Gazette - Mar. 12, 1770

Boston Gazette - Jan. 19, 1778

New England Chronicle - May 18-25, 1775

Pennsylvania Packet - July 8, 1776

The Northwest Ordinance - 1787

The Annapolis Resolution - 1786

Map of the Old Northwest Territory

Currency from the 13 Colonies
Before and during the American Revolution.

Portrait of George Washington

Portrait of Alexander Hamilton

Portrait of James Madison

Thomas Jefferson Announcement - Mar. 1, 1792
Ratification of the Bill of Rights.

Thomas Jefferson's Official Imprint - Mar. 4. 1792
Proposed amendments to the Constitution.

Pennsylvania Packet - Sept. 19. 1787
First public printing of the U. S. Constitution.

ARTIFACTS

John Endecott's Sword
First Governor of the Massachusetts Bay Colony.

Gunsmith's Tool - Circa 1630-50

Spoon - Circa 1630-80

Pair of 18th-Century Pistols

Flintlock Musket
Used during the Revolutionary War.

Powder Horn
Used during the Revolutionary War.

Hunting Sword and Scabbard
Used during the Revolutionary War.

Barrel Canteen
Used during the Revolutionary War.

Inkstand, 1937
Exact replica of the inkstand used by the signers of the Constitution.

Resolution of May 15, 1776
Facsimile.

The Federal Call of Feb. 21, 1787
Facsimile.

COINS

The Brasher Doubloon, 1787
The first gold coin minted in the United States was struck by New York goldsmith Ephraim Brasher in 1787, before there was a U. S. mint. Originally worth $16, the rare coin is today the world's most valuable coin.

Nova Constellatio "Quint" - 1783
This one-of-a-kind silver coin was a pattern for the first proposed United States coinage.

Silver Coin - English, circa 1215
Called a sceat or penny, struck in Canterbury, England.

Now to the issue of funding. Drew Lewis arranged for Fred to meet with the President of American Express. Fred presented the priceless list of materials and explained what he intended to do. Unerring as ever, Fred's radar had found its target. American Express became the lead sponsor of "The Roads to Liberty Tour".

At that point, Fred supervised the donation of approximately $70,000 to the Lincoln Cathedral in England for the right to display the Magna Carta from March 1, to September 11, 1987. Displaying it was one thing. Insuring it was another. Leave it to the ever resourceful Biebel to discover in the course of his research an archaic law that said any object brought into the country on an official visit is automatically insured by the United States of America.

Now the thing about a traveling exhibit is that it needs to be able to travel. How in the world that was going to happen Fred had not yet figured out. He went fishing among all his old contacts and discovered through a friend, Mary Ann Knauss from the Governor's office, there was an old semi-trailer available. It had last been used in the 1970s for a display about former First Lady Eleanor Roosevelt. The State of New York owned it, but Fred was given permission to borrow it.

"My son, Kevin, and I went up on a snowy Friday in a rented tractor with a hitch that we could use to transport the trailer back to Connecticut."

The reason the state had no problem lending the trailer was made clear when they arrived at their destination in Albany. It was badly damaged by neglect and stuck in the mud as well. As the snow fell, Fred and Kevin, (mostly Kevin) proceeded to dig the trailer out. When they finally succeeded in getting it hitched to the tractor, they discovered that the trailer had no brakes.

They inched home in the storm, arriving in Stratford many hours after they had intended. Kevin was an expert with all things mechanical and trucks in particular. He carefully backed the trailer into a heated garage, closed the door and locked it up for the night.

"This is the funny part of that story," said Fred. "On Monday morning, we went over to check out the trailer and the first guy who opened up the door came flying back out, hollering and waving his hands in the air. It turned out that thousands of bees had been hibernating in the old trailer and the heated garage had woken them up." They had to have the entire garage fumigated and cleared of the angry insects.

Kevin got to work stripping the trailer. He ripped out everything, including the roof, and rebuilt the entire thing. The design team included Kevin, the Smithsonian and a number of other historians. They decided the best way to utilize the space was to leverage the already expanded sides of the trailer by filling them with display cabinets so that people could walk through and see the documents. Kevin installed all the lighting, flooring, air-conditioning, humidity controls, and security systems.

The next order of business was to come up with a tractor rig to haul the trailer. Fred spoke with Mark Cannon, the Executive Director of the Bicentennial, and asked who he knew in the auto business. Inspired by the historic significance of the project, Mark's friend, who just happened to be the owner of the Ryder Company, gave them a brand new, specially ordered, $123,000 Peterbilt tractor. It was theirs to use for the entire duration of the Liberty Tour.

Now they had to obtain another truck to transport the special ramps and awnings that would be set up to allow people access inside the truck. There was also a lift for the back of the semi that could accommodate wheelchairs. And they had boxes and boxes of pocket-size copies of the Constitution to give away.

The goal was to kick off the Bicentennial tour in the White House Rose Garden on March 7, 1987. The team had just three months to gather the materials, design and build the displays, the internal security systems, the programs, the presentations, the publicity materials, the schedule of cities and states to be visited, escort security and a thousand other details. No problem. Fred had dealt with deadlines like this many times in his career.

This time, fate intervened. On December 28, 1986, Fred had a debilitating stroke. Lying in his hospital bed, all he could think of was the project he had promised to deliver. Even without the knowledge of what the world would look like twenty years later, he was fully aware that The "Roads to Liberty Tour" was an utterly unique historical event, never to be repeated.

Fred needed a miracle and he got it in the form of his son, Kevin. Stressing and fretting are two of the things you do not want to be doing when you are trying to recover from a stroke. The only way Kevin could keep his father from attempting to crawl on his hands and knees out of the hospital was to order him to hold still and focus on getting well for the opening. Kevin was stepping in and taking over the entire project. Everything would get handled and the deadline would be met. And that is exactly what happened.

Relieved and motivated beyond words, Fred worked double-time at his rehabilitation and therapy. He had to learn to walk and talk all over again. He knew his son was moving mountains to pull off the deadline and he was damned if he wasn't going to be in the Rose Garden with him to share in his triumph.

March 6, 1987, Fred, Violet, Kevin and Jimmy were in Washington to pick up some last minute artifacts from the Smithsonian. Then they brought the beautifully painted, elegant trailer with its new Peterbilt cab, right onto the White House grounds.

The next day, Violet and Fred sat in the front row of the audience as President Reagan and Chief Justice Warren Burger took the platform in the beautiful Rose Garden for the opening ceremonies.

Then it was time to hit the road for the seven-month tour. Their entourage rivaled that of any of today's rock bands. First was the brilliantly painted "Roads To Liberty" semi, followed by the truck that carried the platforms, awnings and wheelchair ramps. Following that were cars that carried four young students who had been specially trained by Fred as docents. They would be the ones who would explain the items in the exhibit and answer questions. There were also vehicles for the crew and back-up drivers.

There were special cars for the Security teams and there were State Police cars--sometimes as many as ten or twelve--that escorted the tour and stayed with them 24/7. Each state used their own troopers, so as the entourage approached a state line, a whole new squad of cars would appear and take over. When the truck was parked for the night, it was the State and local police who stood watch.

One of the unique features of the truck was that it had on board what may have been one of the first GPS systems. Officials could follow the route and knew where the truck was at all times.

There was one particular docent in charge of taking the Magna Carta out of the case every night and locking it into the bullet-proof, bomb-proof case in the bed of the trailer. Fred's grandson, Jimmy, got to be part of the crew for most of the tour through the thirteen colonies. At one point, he was allowed to put on the special white gloves and help the docent move the Magna Carta. Though he was only thirteen, he had learned enough from Fred to know he was holding history in his hands. The experience moved him beyond words.

The Liberty Tour stop at the Alamo in San Antonio, Texas

176

The Liberty Tour was scheduled to visit twenty-six states and one hundred cities. Just as with an election, Fred sent four advance men into each city. They met with mayors and other officials, selected the exhibit sites, briefed authorities on traffic, parking and security issues. The staff who were still working out of Fred's basement took care of booking hotels for all the traveling personnel.

"We didn't know how we would be received until we hit the street. Once we opened at our first location, everybody was overwhelmed by the reaction. It was amazing," Fred says, shaking his head in wonder.

It was summer time; so many days, it was sweltering hot. Other times, there were torrential downpours. People would stand in line for hours to see the amazing exhibit. Only ten people could fit inside at a time, and nobody was ever hurried along or rushed through. By some transcendent grace, the documents appeared to inspire both respect and awe. Waiting in the blazing sun or pouring rain, there was never an instance of vandalism, people were polite and patient with one another. It was as though everybody was there to share this once-in-a-lifetime experience.

Sometimes, they would only be in a city for a weekend; other times, they would stay for a full week. Though he had no idea how huge the turn-out would be, Fred naturally anticipated that there would be lines, so the crew needed to be able to get set up as soon as they reached a location.

Before the tour began, they did what all good roadies do: They practiced. At the local airport in Stratford. Kevin had the whole crew unload the truck, put all the ramps together, assemble the huge wheelchair ramp, and erect the awnings. They would put it together, take it apart, put it together and take it apart. The first attempt took almost half a day. By the time they hit the road, the entire display was ready to open in one hour.

"We had to have it down pat," Jimmy explained, "because, when we came into a city, we would have hundreds, or thousands of people waiting in line to get into this truck. So we were like a stage crew, bang, bang, bang, the truck was set up, and open for business."

When Jimmy said thousands, he wasn't exaggerating. The "Roads to Liberty Tour" was viewed by more than 350,000 individuals. Ten people at a time.

Warren Burger was astonished and hugely gratified by the response the public had to the tour. Additionally, the Commission had printed up and handed out over two million pocket Constitutions. From that point on, Burger started calling Fred, "Admiral of the Roads to Liberty Tour." Then he shortened it to Admiral. So, when the two men got together it was the Chief and the Admiral.

At one point that summer, Fred got a call from the Chief.

"Fred, I just got a letter from Michael Eisner saying that Disney World is going to celebrate their fifteenth anniversary in Florida and they want to tie it in with the Bicentennial.

"They offered to close Disney World to the public, and have all twenty-three members on the Bicentennial Commission, along with celebrities and the press, participate in the celebration. I just wanted you to know I turned them down."

"Why, Chief? I think it's a great idea."

The Chief disagreed. He thought closing down Disney World for the chosen few would be very bad publicity and send the wrong message.

"Chief, you're making a mistake."

"What do you mean?"

"What better place to celebrate America? Are they offering to pick up all the expenses for us and our families?"

"Yes.

"Does that offer include the press, too?"

"Yes."

"So, who is going to criticize us if the press is getting the same VIP treatment? It will be a great experience and it will promote the daylights out of the Bicentennial."

Burger wasn't convinced, so Fred *Biebelized* him by suggesting they meet with the entire Commission and see what they had to say. Guess who won.

The world's largest press party was a gigantic publicity success. Between all of the radio, print and television press, as well as the friends and families of the Bicentennial Commission and invited celebrities, the numbers range from 5,200 to 10,000 people in attendance. The Bicentennial Disney World Extravaganza was splashed all over every media venue.

Sounding just like a ten-year-old kid, Fred remembered, "For three days, everybody could walk into any restaurant and get whatever they wanted to eat or drink. Kids could ride any ride as many times as they wanted and there were shows and balloons and fireworks galore. We even got a group shot of the whole Commission with Mickey Mouse."

The Roads to Liberty Tour Schedule 1987

ILLINOIS
March 15-20
Chicago March 15-18
Springfield March 19-20

WISCONSIN
March 22-28
Madison March 22-23
Milwaukee March 24-25
Appleton March 26
Eau Claire March 27-28

MINNESOTA
March 29- April 3
Minneapolis March 29-30
St. Paul March 31-April 1
Rochester April 2
Duluth April 3

MICHIGAN
April 5-10
Marquette April 5
Sault Ste. Marie April 6
Bay City April 7
Flint April 8
Detroit April 9
Lansing April 10

OHIO
April 12-18
Columbus April 12-13
Marietta April 14
Akron/Canton April 15
Toledo April 16
Cincinnati April 17-18

INDIANA
April 20-24
Indianapolis April 20-22
Evansville April 23-24

IOWA
April 27-28
Des Moines April 27-28

NEBRASKA
April 29-30
Omaha April 29-30

TEXAS
May 3-10
Dallas May 3-4
Austin May 5-6
San Antonio May 7-8
Houston May 9-10

LOUISIANA
May 12-15
Baton Rouge May 12
New Orleans May 13-15

LOUISIANA
May 12-15
Baton Rouge May 12
New Orleans May 13-15

ALABAMA
May16-17
Mobile May 16-17

FLORIDA
May19-29
Tallahassee May 19-20
Orlando/Tampa ay 22-24
Ft. Lauderdale May 25-26
Jacksonville May 28-29

WASHINGTON D.C.
June 1-5
Capitol June 1-2
Pentagon June 3
The Mall June 4-5

DELAWARE
June 7-12
Georgetown une 7-8
Dover June 10
Wilmington June 11-12

NEW JERSEY
June 14-19
Cape May June 14
Trenton June 15-16
Atlantic City une 17
Newark June 18
Stan Hope/Water Loo Village
June 19

PENNSYLVANIA
June 21-26
Harrisburg June 21-22
Erie June 23
Pittsburgh June 24
Allentown June 25
Scranton June 26

CONNECTICUT
June 28-July 4
Hartford June 28-29
Waterbury June 30-July 1
New Haven July 2-3
Bridgeport July 4-5

RHODE ISLAND
July 6-10
Providence July 6
Bristol July 7-8
Newport July 9-11

MASSACHUSETTS
July 12-17
Boston July 12-13
New Bedford uly 14
Lowell July 15
Worcester July 16
Springfield July 17

NEW HAMPSHIRE
July 19-24
Concord July 19-20
Portsmouth July 21
Conway July 22
Hanover July 23

NEW YORK
July 26-31
Albany July 26-27
Syracuse July 28
Niagra Falls July 29
Buffalo July 30-31

GEORGIA
August 2-7
Atlanta August 2-4
Macon August 5
Savannah August 6-7
Augusta August 8

SOUTH CAROLINA
August 9-14
Charleston
Florence
Columbia
Greenville

NORTH CAROLINA
August 16-21
Ashville
Charlotte
Raleigh
Wilmington

VIRGINIA
August 23-28
Yorktown (Victory Ctr.)
August 23-24
Richmond August 25
Roanoke August 26
Charlottesville August 27
Alexandria August 28

MARYLAND
August 30-September 4
Annapolis August 30
Baltimore August 31-Sept 1
Salisbury September 2
Rockville September 3
Hagerstown September 4

NEW YORK
September 6-11
New York City September 6-11

CHAPTER 20
Battle In The Bronx

At a private airport in Tennessee, a horde of angry officials boarded the Governors' private plane. When it landed in Tenafly, New Jersey State troopers joined their Tennessean counterparts, along with an assistant Tennessee Attorney General and a number of other officials. Lights flashing, they headed for the Bronx. They were intent on nailing their quarry, Fred Biebel.

For Fred, the long day was drawing to a close and the sun was setting at Lehman College in the Bronx. He had no idea of what was headed his way. An associate of Fred's, Attorney Norman Liss, had been the one to obtain an original copy of the Declaration of Independence for the exhibit from the State of Maryland. In return, Liss asked that the Tour appear in his home county, the Bronx, and the safest place to do that was Lehman College. The day had been another great success, with students and everybody from the county lining up to view the priceless exhibit. They were just getting ready to close up shop for the night when all hell broke loose.

According to Tom Watson of the Riverdale Press in New York, "The last time the South invaded Northern Territory over states' rights, Robert E. Lee laid siege to a little town 150 miles south of here known as Gettysburg. History repeated itself on Sept. 12 in the Bronx, as an angry horde of Tennesseans stormed the quiet campus of Lehman College to battle the federal government over the Constitution."

Sirens blazing, the vehicles disgorged an irate State Museum Director, two members of her staff, Tennessee State Troopers, New York State Troopers, an Assistant State Attorney General, the Very Reverend Oliver Fiennes, dean of England's Lincoln Cathedral, and an assistant of his, in addition to what the Tennessean called a "gun-toting platoon of New York City police officers."

"A whole entourage of people arrived" Fred was quoted as saying, "like it was the Brink's robbery or something. They blocked off all the entrances and demanded documents we had every intention of giving them." Someone from the Sheriff's office approached and demanded to know who was in charge.

"That would be me," declared Fred. "What the hell is going on?"

"We have an order to show cause why Supreme Court Justice of Bronx County, Judge Anita Florio, directed my office to search for and seize the copy of the Bill of Rights that had been owned by Thomas Jefferson and was presented to the State of Maryland.

"We are suing you because we have the obligation to search for this document and represent the State of Tennessee because they have an exhibition which they plan to start displaying tomorrow to commemorate their celebration of the United States Constitution."

"Are you nuts?" Fred demanded. "Do you know which Supreme Court justice is in charge of this federal exhibit? I say Chief Justice Warren Burger trumps your Judge Florio any day."

The entire furor was created by a simple scheduling error that had been made three years earlier. The State of Tennessee had an agreement to display Jefferson's original proposal for twelve amendments to the Constitution, The Bill of Rights, and a letter signed by Jefferson. They had also made a $34,000 deposit for the same copy of the Magna Carta that was on the Liberty Tour.

Unfortunately, the dates had overlapped. The Liberty Tour was headed for the big finale in Philadelphia. The first Fred heard of the conflict of dates was three weeks earlier. At that point, he had requested permission to keep the documents for several extra days-- because he wanted to keep the exhibit intact--for the official day of celebration in Philadelphia. The museum director said no.

Fred had no choice but to agree to turn the documents over. However, he made it clear that he was under contract, not to mention that he had given his word, that nobody but the Smithsonian would be allowed to remove the documents.

The next thing he knew, he was under assault and all exit routes were blocked by flashing police cars and armed men. A crowd had gathered and the whole scene had taken on a surreal quality. They battled back and forth for hours. Threats to confiscate the documents were met with challenges to prove the right to do so. The Sheriff insisted that he had a legal restraining order, backed by a search and seizure order. Attorney Liss fought back, saying that the state did not have the right to sue or search anyone or anything, under the current circumstances.

Finally, around midnight, the Sheriff insisted he was going to arrest Fred, search the truck and take the papers. "Like hell," responded Biebel. Fred may not have had the clout to call President Reagan whenever he felt like it--but he had the power to get the Chief Justice of the Supreme Court out of bed in the middle of the night--and that's just what he did.

Burger spoke to Attorney Liss and after getting all the details, said, "Norman, don't your judges in the Bronx know they can't sue the United States of America? This is a U.S. exhibition and we are a U.S. Commission. You better work it out with them, otherwise, I'm going to call the governor and there is going to be a big problem." Privately, Burger wondered if Tennessee was merely staging a publicity stunt.

Liss repeated the Chief Justice's words about not being able to sue the U.S. government, at which point the Sheriff said he was going to arrest Fred.

"With that," says Attorney Liss, "Fred stormed into the truck, closed the door and locked himself in, putting his body between the officials and the documents. He was adamant that no one could take any of the documents unless it was someone from the Smithsonian Institution."

After a lot of bluff and bluster on both sides, around 2 o'clock in the morning, the Tennessee contingent finally agreed to sign a document. They assumed complete accountability and responsibility for any damage done to any of the documents during the transfer, or while in their possession.

Fred became apoplectic when he heard that Tennessee claimed that he and the Chief Justice and the Bicentennial Commission had intentionally conspired to withhold the documents and not honor Tennessee's contract.

He hauled them into Court, with Attorney Liss representing the Commission. Calling the state's actions illegal and the judge's restraining order ludicrous, the Commission wanted payment to cover legal expenses incurred.

Fred got his way. The State of Tennessee acknowledged its mistake, the Governor wrote a letter of apology and paid damages in the amount of $1.00.

Citizens, be warned. You do not, under any circumstances, want to mess with Frederick K. Biebel when he has given someone his word.

CHAPTER 21
Read Them Their Rights

In 1985, yet another British Man of War manifested in Fred's world. Counting the one that originally kidnapped Robert Hatch, then the HMS Frolic that likely had "impressed" Hatch's son--and possibly the HMS Poicitiers to which the U.S. Wasp had to surrender--then adding the one that joined the brig in pursuit of the Alligator up the Stone River by the Wappoo Cut--the total comes to five. But, who's counting?

Perhaps it was Fate's way of attempting to make things right when the last appearance of the specter ship turned into a gift for Fred and all the people who would come to know her.

Regardless of whether you believe in reincarnation, Fred Biebel, Doc Gunther, and Kaye Williams, who owns Captain's Cove in Bridgeport, have been pals for centuries. They've known one another in this lifetime for over fifty years. Each man is utterly indomitable in spirit. Each has been a unique visionary. They are all stubborn as mules, can't hold still, and won't give up or give in without a fight. They also like to smoke cigars and take on impossible projects that will sap their energies, tax their patience and make money for people other than themselves.

Back in 1984, Doc Gunther's help was required in an official capacity. Kaye Williams had bought a wreck of a replica of the HMS Rose that was moored to the side of a dock in Rhode Island.

The original British war ship was scuttled by her crew in 1779 in a narrow channel off Savannah, Georgia, to block access to the harbor. The replica of the Rose was in terrible disrepair, but Kaye could see she was still seaworthy. Apparently, the Coast Guard got a little cranky and tried to stop Kaye from towing the boat he'd paid $75,000 for to Bridgeport. Senator Gunther stepped in and smoothed over the waters.

Over the years, Fred had helped Kaye, along with a huge number of volunteers, to restore the Rose.

"I made a promise to Kaye Williams," Fred explained. "I told him when I first started the Magna Carta project that I would bring it to Captain's Cove on the 4th of July." Fred, Doc and Kaye were all there when Fred made good on his promise, as was half the city of Bridgeport and a good portion of the State of Connecticut.

Ironically, the English Magna Carta and HMS Rose were the star attractions celebrating American Independence in Connecticut that 4th of July.

Several years later, Fred and Kaye were sitting at the Cove one day and Fred found himself staring at the Rose. "I was just thinking about her history and then the Liberty Tour popped into my head and I said, 'you know what, Kaye? Maybe we ought to do something like the Liberty Tour with the Rose.'

"We talked about it and decided we should celebrate the Bill of Rights. So then it became a matter of whether I could get access to it again."

As always, money was the first consideration so Fred went "fishing". The New York Phone Company was beguiled by his presentation and became the main sponsor of the Bill of Rights tour. Warren Burger also authorized financial support from the Bicentennial Commission.

With that piece in place, Fred went back to the people he had met at the Smithsonian through the Chief. They provided a number of artifacts from the museum and Kaye Williams contributed several items from the original HMS Rose that had been recovered from her watery grave. Then, they went to work building a special housing that would protect the precious document from humidity and salt air.

At the same time, Kaye was working to get the HMS Rose named as an official sailing school vessel, so she undertook several tours. The first one was just about showcasing the ship and earning her 'sea miles'. She headed up to Nova Scotia and then did a tour of the Great Lakes. Once again, Fred's grandson, Jimmy, got to go along. He spent his entire summer climbing the rigging, working the giant sails, and taking his turn on watch.

At one point, when the Rose was in Chicago, Fred joined the tour to see how things were going. He was amazed and impressed by his sixteen year old grandson, as he watched him fly around the rigging with complete confidence fifty feet off the deck, working the big sails. It crossed his mind that he could have been watching Robert Hatch or Hatch's son aboard a British vessel more than two hundred years earlier.

Finally, in 1991, the HMS Rose began her historical tour. She sailed the East Coast from Maine to Florida while displaying Rhode Island's original draft of the Bill of Rights.

Just as with the Liberty Tour, Fred had advance teams handle the logistics and planning. They would sail into port, there would be a reception on board for local dignitaries and, the following day, they would be open for business.

The Rose was a big draw because she was such an unusual and dramatic sight as she appeared on the horizon and sailed into port. Each time they approached a major city, they would be escorted by every type of pleasure and sailing craft imaginable. Everybody wanted to see the tall ship with all her sails unfurled.

Fred Biebel at the helm of the H.M.S. Rose

H.M.S. Rose

Then she would tie up dock side, and the crowds would be waiting to come on board, view the ship, and read The Bill of Rights. Once aboard, nearly everyone expressed shock at the limited and cramped size of the living quarters below decks. People marveled that an entire crew of men could be at sea for months at a time in such conditions, never mind what it must have been like during a battle. The public received an education in the hardships versus romantic presentation of war and life aboard a nineteenth-century vessel.

"It was really exciting because we had the drama of sea travel in addition to housing a precious piece of American History," Fred recalls. "Don't forget, we were a sailing vessel, but we still had deadlines and a schedule to meet. We had storms and rough weather, and we had to work with the tides because the dock tie-ups had to be specially created.

189

"I remember one night we had a reception in New York City at the South Street Sea Port. Every politico and dignitary within fifty miles had shown up. All of a sudden, a huge squall blew up the river and we had the worst thunder and lightening storm. Everybody had to get below decks. It was as if we were trying to win a contest about how many people we could stuff in a phone booth.

"Most places below decks, a grown man can't stand fully upright anyhow, so now we have all these people mashed together with all hell breaking loose above us. The ship was bobbing and swaying and tugging at her spring-lines and you could hear the wind screaming in the rigging." Fred was laughing. "It was probably the best day of the whole damn tour."

CHAPTER 22
Political Afterlife

In 1987, Fred decided he might like to work in the private sector. A number of his fellow politicos had made the move from public to private life and they were all quite happy with their choices.

His years in the political trenches had made him a master fundraiser and an organizer of epic proportions. However, rather than jump into the corporate world, he wanted to be able to leverage his abilities to do some good in the world. All he needed was to decide where and for whom he could apply his talents.

After years of commuting back and forth to Washington D. C. and puddle-jumping across the United States, Fred was looking for a more local challenge.

Of course, he quickly tapped a few friends for letters of recommendation that certainly would startle any organization that needed an introduction to Fred: The Honorable Warren E. Burger, (Chief Justice, retired); The Honorable George Bush, Vice President, White House; Dr. Lynne V. Cheney, Chairman National Endowment for the Humanities; The Honorable Christopher Dodd, United States Senate; Mr. Lionel Hampton, Ambassador for Music to the World; The Honorable Edward M. Kennedy, United States Senate; The

Honorable Drew Lewis, CEO, Union Pacific Corporation; The Honorable William O'Neill, Governor, State of Connecticut; Mr. S. Bruce Smart, Undersecretary of Commerce for International Trade, and a host of others.

Fred still had energy to burn, but was not certain what step to take. He created a start-up business and sold it, but was still on the lookout for new opportunities.

It has often been said that 'life is what happens when you're busy making other plans.' For Fred, that statement became operative when he was tapped by Connecticut Governor John Rowland to do some business outreach for the state Department of Labor. As a result of that assignment, Fred's was named director of the Governor's Office in Southwestern Connecticut.

Now that he was back in Connecticut, he also couldn't say, "No" to the many local non-profit and community groups that sought his help.

Perhaps the United Way of Eastern Fairfield County summed it up best when they presented an award to Fred for his service to the Kennedy Center, a local non-profit serving people with disabilities and special needs: "Frederick K. Biebel (Governor's Southwestern Office) is a prime example of an outstanding Community Builder. Throughout his career, Fred has worked extensively to revitalize cities, states and the citizens who reside within them. As a member of The Kennedy Center, Inc.'s Board of Directors, Nominating Committee Chair and member of several other committees, Fred Biebel has brought a wealth of knowledge, experience and network contacts. Fred Biebel is an invaluable advocate."

Fred's ability to orchestrate fundraising efforts and then conduct the festivities with style grew out of his political experience. Born in Bridgeport, Fred had apparently inherited the gifts of the city's greatest impresario, the legendary P.T. Barnum. In fact, his work and Barnum's legacy would come together in a moment of serendipity that has delighted generations of Connecticut residents.

Back in 1948, when Fred was working at D M Read's, his boss, Sidney Reisman, was a member of the Chamber of Commerce. One evening, Reisman got bogged down with business and asked Fred to attend the meeting as his stand-in and take notes for him.

For her outstanding contribution to World War II, The City of Bridgeport became known as "the Arsenal of Democracy". The meeting that night was to consider how best to honor the people who had worked so tirelessly for the war effort. It was time for a celebration.

It was decided that very night that they would create an ongoing annual festival that would feature different activities and celebrations throughout the year. They named it The Barnum Festival in honor of the famous showman and mayor of Bridgeport. Each year, a special citizen would be awarded the title of Ringmaster and he or she would conduct all the ceremonial events during the year of their reign.

As he dutifully noted all the details that night, Fred had no way of knowing that, forty-two years later, he would be chosen as Ringmaster. (By now, we hardly need note the ever-present coincidence factor or that it was over four decades in the making).

The year of his reign, 1990, Fred's six-year-old granddaughter, Jaime, got to go with him to the big Barnum Parade. Jaime worshipped her grandfather and was as excited as only a six-year-old can be-- promising to be with Fred for every Parade. She sat proudly in the car next to him and waved to the crowds. Like Fred, once Jaime makes a commitment to something, she keeps it. Fred remained active in the Barnum Festival, so Jaime would even leave college to come home and join him for festival events. It's been eighteen years now and she hasn't missed a single year.

In 2006, as has become the custom, Bruce and Freddie also rode in the big parade car. That year, however, it was Jaime driving the honorary vehicle.

Fred also remains a huge supporter of the Junior Olympics, which originally began as a Jaycee project.

Fred Biebel as Barnum Festival Ringmaster

Ostensibly, Fred formally retired in 2005. At least, they had a huge retirement celebration and dinner, but those who know Fred well realized that retirement was not really an option for this man who seemed to even work in his sleep. Scaling back, maybe, but going fishing was out of the question.

Fred remains active on numerous boards and in countless community activities. In 2007, he and his Co-chairman, Dorothy Larson, helped raise over a million dollars for the Kennedy Fund, which has benefited people of all ages with disabilities and special needs.

In April 2008, Christopher Healey, Republican Chairman of Connecticut, put the icing on the cake of Fred's official non-retirement, when he announced that Fred would serve as an at-large delegate at the Republican National Convention. Mr. "B" will be back in action at the Minneapolis Republican National Convention during the first week of September, 2008. That makes a streak of fourteen National conventions in a row.

CHAPTER 23
There Are No Words

There are no words to describe what came next. Well, in a manner of speaking, there are. As told by those in the context of the extraordinary exchange.

A few quick notes first. Five days before this book was to be finished, Fred went to the funeral of a relative. There he ran into his cousin, Nancy Hatch Warner. He mentioned the book and the fact that Robert Hatch was going to be in it. She told him about a story that had happened three years earlier.

More specifically, about an intriguing email that she had received from a young man in Charleston, South Carolina, Thursday, July 14, 2005:

Hello:

To begin with, let me say that I am an archaeologist who is working his way through graduate school at a salvage yard (this sets the back drop).

Today, while I was at work a person came to the yard to get a transmission. While we were helping them load the transmission into their truck I noticed a large piece of stone upon which I could make out the date 1814. I asked them about it and they claimed that they found it in their yard and were going to use it to fill a hole. As an archaeologist, I could not let this happen so I talked them into letting me have the stone so that I could find if the person listed had any living descendants.

The stone (the top half that they had) belongs to a Captain Robert Hatch who died at the age of 56 in 1814. The stone says that he suffered a mortal wound and died in a month ending in "uary". Since I live in the Charleston, SC area this sure sounds like the Captain Robert Hatch whose obituary you have listed on your genealogy page.

I just wanted the descendants to know what I stumbled upon today. A man of the caliber of Captain Hatch should have his stone repatriated. So, I am writing to ask you what I should do. If your family wants it and can arrange a manner to ship it, I will let you have it (as it rightfully would belong to you). If you know the provenience of his grave I will contact the appropriate county so that the stone can be once again with the grave. Or, If you want I will donate the stone to the local historical society or museum. To think that someone was going to use such a historical piece as fill for a hole is preposterous.

I will eagerly await your response so that I can fulfill your wishes on what to do with the stone.

Best Regards,
James Curry

PS. If this is not the Robert Hatch to which your family is related could you please, if you know, refer me to the appropriate family.

This was Nancy Hatch Warner's initial response to James.

James,

Thanks so much. I will need to think about this. I will get back to you.

Nancy

To which James responded the following day.

Nancy,

I will keep it in a secure location until I hear from you as to what to do with it. I am sure that it was an unexpected event.

Sincerely,
James Curry

Nancy got in touch with a relative named Charlotte who, in turn, took the step of contacting her cousin, Hale Sweeney, in North Carolina. Hale wrote to James the very next day.

Dear Mr. Curry

Captain Robert Hatch was my paternal great, great-grandfather. He died as a result of wounds he received in a battle with British ships in the river near the Wapoo cut. He had been a ship master all his life and was engaged in coastal trade, mostly between New England and Charleston, from the time he moved to Charleston in the early 1790s until the War of 1812 began. He volunteered his services in that war and was appointed Sailing Master (in charge of all sails and setting of the sails, etc.) on board the schooner Alligator, a privateer.

I was raised in Charleston, on Broad Street, and went to the Bethel Street Methodist Church on Calhoun Street. Capt. Hatch was buried there. Every time I came out of Sunday School through the back door, I would come out right next to his grave and would frequently stop and reread the inscription, chiseled in those small letters. I also was a Sea Scout in Charleston, and was instrumental in seeing that we named our Sea Scout ship, the Alligator, after his ship.

Somewhere in the 60s, Bethel tore down the old Sunday School Building to make room for a new building, and at the same time dug up a lot of the tomb stones and put them under the old Boy Scout building. (About their treatment of the tombstones, I've frequently thought that you just can't trust churches with something sacred like tombstones! (smile). I tried to get their janitor/yard man to dig it out from under the old Boy Scout Building and offered money, but he said it was too much work!)

I would LOVE to have it and would promise to care for it and to see that it was finally in the possession of some group, like a museum or historical group, who would appreciate its relation to Charleston history.

You may reach me at this email address, or send me mail or call me. We will be coming to Charleston soon (to try out the new bridge and to visit relatives) and in any event I would like to come by and see the tombstone.

Hale Sweeny

Ever the professional, James Curry wanted to make sure Nancy knew that he had been contacted by another member of the family and promptly emailed her.

Hello:

I just wanted to forward to you a copy of an e-mail I received from Hale Sweeny. If this is the wishes of the family then the Sweeny family is more than welcome to what is rightfully theirs. I just wanted to double check with you, my main point of contact on this matter, to ensure that it is what the family wants.

Thank you,
James Curry

Then he responded to Hale.

Hello:

You are more than welcome to the stone which is rightfully the property of your family. The story of how it was removed from its original location is somewhat depressing....on the positive side at least there are laws now to help protect such items.

When you come to the area feel free to stop by to get it. My address is North Charleston, SC. I can also be reached via telephone.

On a more personal note, my fiancee's grandmother, Mrs. Frances Melton (maiden name was Robinson), was curious as to where your family lived on Broad Street and if you were any relation to the Sweeny's that had the pharmacy.

I will keep the stone protected and will wait to hear from you so that we can arrange to have it repatriated back into your family.

Thanks for the great information.
Sincerely,
James Curry

As the wife of a minister, Nancy was relieved and happy to know that Hale would take care of Captain Hatch's gravestone.

James,

This sounds great! Charlotte contacted Hale and this seems most appropriate! Thanks so much.

Nancy

Mr. Sweeny,

I apologize for delay in my getting a picture to you. I have attached a photo of the section of the tombstone we have to this e-mail. I look forward to speaking with you again.

Sincerely,
James Curry

James,

Thanks a bunch for the photograph. Yes, that is the tombstone as I
remember it - or at least about one fifth of it! It was quite long - long
enough to cover the grave - and had the entire story of the fight between
the Alligator and the British Ships and barges engraved on the stone. I
do have a copy of the words from the entire stone, but have not yet
found it in my records. When I find it, I will scan it and send it to you.
Looking forward to meeting you.

Hale

Hi:

Nancy, in case Hale did not have a chance to forward the picture, I have
attached it to this e-mail.

James

James,

Thanks. It is amazing to me that these graves were treated in such a
way--I had no idea!

Nancy

That was the last correspondence James had with any member of the
family. He tried contacting Hale by phone, but to no avail. He had
promised Hale he would keep the stone safe and that is precisely
what he did. Then, three years later, out of the blue, he received the
following:

James,

I don't know if you are still at this email address. My cousin Fred Biebel
from Stratford CT is having a book written about him which includes
Captain Robert Hatch. Hale Sweeney has died. Do you know about the
whereabouts of the tombstone? Hale's son thinks that he had gotten
too sick to come down to get it.

Nancy

Hello!

Thank you for that update. I had been wondering for a while what had happened to Mr. Sweeny as he was never able to make it here to pick up the stone.

I contacted the Charleston Museum about adding it to their collection, but they never really gave a definitive answer other than they did not know if they had room (physical space) in their repository for it.

So, I do still have it just as I found it a couple years ago and was hoping someday someone would contact me again about it as I really do want it with its rightful family members.

James Curry

I will leave to others the explanation of this most recent and extraordinary series of coincidences. If I had scripted this story, people would have rolled their eyes skyward and scoffed.

What are the chances that an archaeology student would be loading a transmission in a truck, in a salvage yard, spot a gravestone in the rubble of the pickup's bed, and ask to take possession of it?

Who else would possibly have recognized the value of the broken, faded stone?

Add to that the fact that James took the time to track the family, double-checked to make sure that it was acceptable for Sweeney to take possession of the stone and then, when he failed to claim it, kept it safe for years until it could find its way home.

Only in Fred Biebel's world would you find a professional with such integrity and respect. I'd say that Robert Hatch knew what he was doing when he chose a man of James' caliber to guard his history and his heritage.

Oh yes. As it turns out, James was working at the salvage yard as a computer consultant. He just happened to be available when a worker called up to the office to see if anyone could give him a hand lifting a heavy transmission.

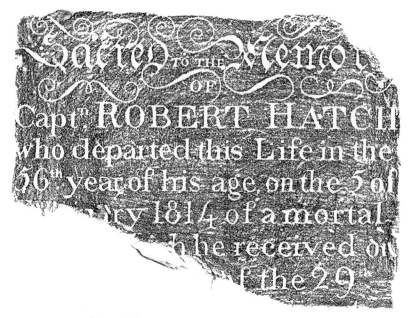

Rubbing of the gravestone portion made by James Curry

One more thing. James' in-laws live on Edgewater Island in Charleston which finds its main separation from land due to the Wappoo Cut. In fact, you have to take Wappoo Drive to get to their home.

Call it what you will: chance, Synchronicity, luck, quirkiness, unique planet alignment, fluke, whatever. The fact remains that Fred and Robert have a lot in common. They were honest and kind. Cared about their families. Fought for what they believed in. Served their countries. Refused to give up and give in.

There is much to be learned from those who fought behind the scenes. Which is the reason that a life-long, heart-strong, avowed Democrat, wrote this paean. To a Republican.

EPILOGUE

Robert Hatch's tombstone will finally be given the respect it deserves when it is displayed in a museum.

Who knows? Captain Hatch appears to be quite as ingenious as Fred Biebel. Maybe the missing pieces of his history as represented on his gravestone will also reappear in time.

FREDERICK K. BIEBEL

Frederick K. Biebel, "Mr. B" has spent sixty years of political life beginning with service as a Town Councilman and a fourteen-year term as Republican Town Chairman of Stratford, CT. He has served as Deputy Republican National Chairman and the liaison to the White House during President Ronald Reagan's term of office, Chairman of the Connecticut Republican State Central Committee and Chairman of all fifty state Republican Chairmen. Mr. B has worked for six Republican President and has attended fourteen Republican National Conventions. Active on many boards in his community, he is a 50-year member of the America St. John's Lodge #8AF & AM , The National Society of the Sons of the Revolution (SAR), and the Shriners of North America. He is also a Deacon of Lordship Community Church of Stratford, CT. He and his wife, Violet, are the parents of three grown children, seven grandchildren and four great grandchildren.

2008 Family Tree

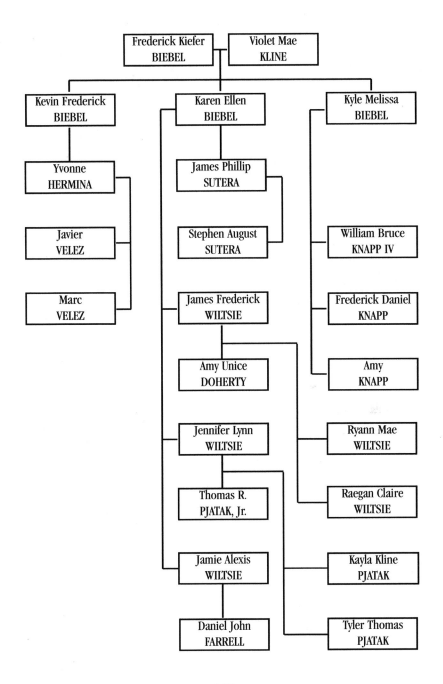

SUSAN HELLER

In a previous life Susan Heller was a writer/director and novelist. She now works as a media consultant, speech writer and author. She has collaborated on a number of books and ghost writes biographies and articles.